YOUNG WRITERS

OVER THE MOON

WEST YORKSHIRE

published in Great Britain in 1996 by
POETRY NOW
1-2 Wainman Road, Woodston,
Peterborough, PE2 7BU

HB ISBN 1 86188 009 X
SB ISBN 1 86188 004 9

Foreword

The *Over The Moon* competition was an overwhelming success - over 43,000 entries were received from 8-11 year olds up and down the country, all written on a wide variety of subjects. Reading all these poems has been a painstaking task - but very enjoyable.

Many of the poems were beautifully illustrated. This just emphasises how much time, effort and thought was put into the work. For me, this makes the editing process so much harder.

I hope that *Over The Moon West Yorkshire* highlights the diversity of today's young minds. I believe that each of these poems shows a great deal of creativity and imagination. Many of them also express an imagination. Many of them also express an understanding of the problems, socially and environmentally, that we are all facing.

The poems that follow are all written on different levels, and some are more light-hearted than others. With a considerable variety of subjects and styles, there should be something to appeal to everyone.

Sarah Andrew
Editor

CONTENTS

Holy Name Primary School

Rachel Goodyear	58
Laura Harvey	59
Roseanna Dowe	59

Hopton Junior, Infant & Nursery School

Rachel Lyons	60
Melanie Brooke	60
Luke Wilson	61

Hothfield Street Junior School

James Laycock	62
Helen Rishworth	62
Emily Needham	63
Peter Gunn	63
Joanne McLoughlin	64
Michelle Starmer	64
Carla Pearson	65
Suzanne Cuthbert	65
Lisa Meehan	66
Dawn Wigglesworth	66
Fiona Bowden	67
Laura Clark	67
Rachel Wallbank	68
Ben Cartledge	68
Laura Whitely Smith	69
Amber Louise Smale	70
Rebecca Steeples	71
Jack Weeden	71
Luke Arrowsmith	72
Jenny Ross	72
Katie Harrison	73
Lucy Peel	73
Simon Heath	74
Jenny Tate	75
Nicola Robinson	76
Leanne Wainwright	77
Gwen Needham	78

Keighley Preparatory School

Jemima Olivia Robinson	78
Johanna Weston	79

Kingsway Primary School

Rachael Kirby	80
Gemma Walton	80
Rachael Greaves	81
Simon Newton	81
Jade Shaw	82
Jamie Greenway	82
Andrew Longfield	83
Mark Holgate	83
Jennifer Marston	84
Leigh Clarkson	84
Lindsay Martin	85

Kippax Greenfield Primary School

Lyndsey Farish	85
Leanne Beever	86
Richard Ratcliffe	86
Rebecca Lamb	87

Larks Hill J & I School

Claire Mitchell	87
Teresa Speakman	88
Stevie-Ann Harrison	88
Rebecca Walker	89
Danielle Knee	89
Amit Patel	90
Steven Barrow	90
James Shaw	91
Natalie Seddon	91
James Stott	92
Robert Nowak	92
Matthew Thrall	93
Natalie Guy	93
Faye Sidaway	94
Jack Storr	94
Ashley Hewes	95

Lightcliffe C of E School

Stephen Bryden	95
Natalie Thorn	96
Maxine Harrop	96
David Kemp	97
Matthew Broadbent	97
Sarah Cadman	98
Laurette Zarneh	99
Amie Horne	99
Daniel Seekings	100
Laura Newby	100
Chloe Leanne Cox	101
Victoria Stobart	102
Suzanne McQueen	102
Elizabeth Johnson	103
Natalie McCamley	104
Mark Nowoslawski	105
Rebecca Haigh	105
Emma Jane Robinson	106
Jimmy Smallwood	107
Rebecca Riley	107
Sophie Bowyer	108
Grey Hawtin	108
Rachel Naylor	109
Alexis J Lea	109
Robert Young	110
Gareth Kitson	111
Abigail Brooke	111
Thomas Harling	112
Mark Griffiths	112
Sophie Angelica Thomas	113

Luddenden Dene J & I School

Tracy Wormald	114
Lucy Crane	114
Jodie Platt	115
Jenny Grant	116
Chris Halstead	117

Manningham Middle School

Mount St Mary's RC Primary School

Parkinson Lane J & I School

Queen's Road J & I School

Katherine McBurnie	191
Amy Carrigan	192
Jade Scullion	193
Catherine Sanderson	194
Jennifer Moore	194
Sally Fowler	195
Paula Woollin	195

Talbot Primary School

Hannah Farnfield	196
Adele Hurst	196

Thornhill J & I School

Emma Victoria Brandwood	197
Stacey Helliwell	198

Walton Junior School

Lauren Carter	198
Laura Simonite	199

Wellington Middle School

Emma Hudson	199
David Langwade	200
Paul Bryar	200
Alison Epton	201
Adele Fieldhouse	202
Katie Flathers	202
Josie Crossland	203
Kiranjeet Kaur	204
Sara Hibbitts	204
Gavin Stowell	205

Woodend Middle School

Bryony Betts	206
Samantha Wardle	206
Daniel Hoyle	207
Stuart Gray	208
Racheal Ann Grogan	208
Amanda Worrall	209
Amy Axon	210
Danielle Phillips	211
Amanda Fish	211
Abigail Dewhirst	212

SNOW

Snow is like clouds,
floating from the sky.

It is like flour,
being poured out of the heavens.

Snow is like a white carpet,
laid out on the ground.

It is like white paint,
being kicked all over the street.

Snow is like plastic bags,
floating down from the angels.

It is like milk,
that has been spilt.

Snow is like cotton wool,
being thrown from the clouds.

It is like rubbers,
being shaken off the tree.

Snow is like pepper,
being thrown from the roof.

It is like socket switches,
that have been broken.

Cassandra L Bibb (10) Ackton Pastures J & I School

LIFE

Birds that fly in the sky.
Children that play merrily.
The sun that shines in the sky.
Whilst mums and dads are sitting around
Eating steak and kidney pie.

Saffron Smith (8) Ackton Pastures J & I School

MY PET PIRANHA

My pet piranha isn't very bliss,
But if you have some homework,
Just remember this.
When you go to school the next day,
Just say to the teacher,
My piranha ate it miss.
One day I went to school with
Scratches on my face,
My clothes were torn,
Miss sat me in my place,
She asked me what happened,
I said my piranha,
Tried to eat me miss.
It jumped down the toilet and,
Terrorised the town
It ate school children
And a king with a crown
      Till one day
          It went
               Pop!

Elizabeth Paton (10) Bowling Green J & I School

MONSTERS

Monsters are scary things,
They will eat you all up.
So if you see one run for your life,
And so if he gets you stab it with a knife.
If he jumps on your bed,
Slap him round the head,
Now you know what they're like,
Their horrible habits,
So if you see one,
You know what to do.
Just give them a fright.

Peter Ibbetson (9) Bowling Green J & I School

MY PET TIGER

My pet tiger is pink and orange and blue,
He can disguise himself as a cow that goes moo,
Or an old shoe,
My pet tiger can disguise itself as you,
And a pig too,
So if you hear a painful roar,
It's my tiger he's broken his jaw,
If you hear his nasty roar,
Feed him, he likes his meat raw!

Victoria Cattan (9) Bowling Green J & I School

THE HAUNTED TRAIN!

As I get on the haunted train,
I feel a shiver go down my spine.
The haunted train goes bumpety bump,
Along the haunted line.
A skeleton jumps out in front of me,
Agggh, there it is again!
When you're on the haunted train,
You're going down a haunted lane.
Bumpety bump, I'm shaking all over,
Daylight again!
Never go on the haunted train!

Jenna Milner (10) Bowling Green J & I School

THE NIGHT OF THE SKELETONS

Tingle tingle rattle rattle,
The graveyard comes to life.
The soil crumbles beneath your feet,
As bony fingers reach.
The dead pull themselves from out their graves,
And just stand there staring.
Their eye sockets empty,
Blackness creeps around you as they start to walk.
They march and march their footsteps crumbling,
They slowly slowly walk.
Then they turn round as I start to scream,
Then they walk back to their bed.
And I return home to rest my head.

Amy Smith (9) Bowling Green J & I School

4

WHEN DID GOD?

When did God make the planets?
When did God make the sea?
When did God make the elephant?
When did God make me?

When did God make the fishes?
When did God make the flea?
When did God make sealife?
And when did God make you and me?

Deborah J Redhead (9) Bowling Green J & I School

A DAY ON THE FARM

Up at six,
  eyes are red,
  can't even get up out of bed.

    Breakfast ready
  eat it up,
  happy now.
  Work till noon,
  feed the cows their lunch,
  ted the hay for the rest of the day:
  Balers bust. Full of rust.
  In at eight, I can't wait till
  tomorrow . . . snore, snore, snore.

Joshua Sheard (10) Bowling Green J & I School

MY BROTHER BABOON

My brother comes out of the zoo.
He is a tall skinny baboon.
He's good at footie.
When he gets home he jumps and runs around all day.
But all my brother is is a tall skinny baboon.

He eats as fast as a pig.
He runs as fast as a cheetah.
He jumps as high as a kangaroo.
But all my brother is is a tall skinny baboon.

When he speeds to school and back.
He comes home like a kangaroo.
But all my brother is is a tall skinny baboon.

Jeanette Gayton (10) Broomwood Middle School

MY MUM

My mum's hair is like a zebra's fur,
her eyes are like the sea,
mum's ears are as small as a mouse.

Her legs are as fat as elephant's legs,
a nose as big as a hedgehogs,
a mouth like a tiger's mouth.

When she's cross she stamps her
feet as loud as thunder.

James Coe (10) Broomwood Middle School

MY BROTHER

Hair like a hedgehog
Teeth like sparkling champagne
Eyes like stars
A nose like a boxer
A mouth that smiles
Gentle but strong
Always so cool.

James Johnson (10) Broomwood Middle School

L'ESCARGOT

A body like a slug,
It's a mobile home,
It slithers like a snake,
A spiral shell like an ammonite,
Glue follows it,
Tentacles like knitting needles,
As slow as a cloud.

Kelly Greenwood (10) Broomwood Middle School

L'ESCARGOT

As lazy as the clouds,
As light as a feather,
With a mobile home,
It's as slow as ever,
With a slimy trail,
It's as dead as the weather.

Tracey Cronshaw (10) Broomwood Middle School

GPB (GREATEST POSSIBLE BEING)

Brain like Mr Heeley,
Ears like Miss Limb,
As strong as an ox,
As cunning as a fox,
Muscles like boxes,
Smells like *toxic waste!*
Fingers like paste,
Solid as a wall,
Can batter all,
Nose like a hall,
Surfs on a cloud,
An elephant is as loud,
Always fussy so attracts a crowd.

Shaun Cockcroft (10) Broomwood Middle School

MY SISTER

She laughs like a hyena.
Hair like string.
As gentle as a lamb.
As quiet as a fish.
Ears like mushrooms.
She's as small as a pony.
As thin as a stick.
She sings like a bird.
She's as good as a pig.
Her fingers are as small as twigs.
Her feet are like a lion's.
My sister smiles like the sun.

Jon Hodson (10) Broomwood Middle School

OLD GRANNIES

My gran changed into a tortoise because she's really slow.
Then suddenly she was growing snow out of her head.
Her face became a Yorkshire pudding.

She had hairy legs that became ostrich legs.
Her nose was all crinkled and her nose
became an old china cup.

She has cheeks like roses
She's as gentle as a puppy and
she's started growing fingers
like a Roald Dahl witch.

Her eyes are like the sea glistening
and she's sweet like sugar.
She always likes company
especially me.

Lisa Kyte (9) Broomwood Middle School

BIG

I wish I was huge,
I wish I was massive,
immense, tremendous.
I wish I was vast bulking
mountainous mammoth;
I wish I was hulking gigantic
fat colossal spacious;
I wish I was stout;
But really I am; small.

Adrian Hewitt (10) Broomwood Middle School

MYSELF

I am a chimpanzee as loud as
Carl.
As strong as an ox,
A budding Arnold
Shwazzeneger.
Feet as smelly as skunks,
As friendly as a dolphin.
As versatile as a Birdseye
potato waffle,
A Linford Christie with rocket
shoes.
A mental, massive, muscle man
who's as daft as a clown.

Joshua Briggs (9) Broomwood Middle School

MY GRANDAD

My grandad is grumpy
like a bear with a sore head.
He laughs like a hyena, and
eats like a pig.
His nose is like Pinnochio's.
His mouth is like a hippo's mouth.
His muscles are like a pile of
cardboard boxes.

Thomas Burton (10) Broomwood Middle School

MY RELATIONS

A musician made my Uncle Frank because
his bed is like a case and he plays the guitar like a mad man!

A story writer made my mum because
she's always reading books or magazines!

A chef made my dad because
he is big like a loaf of bread, he rises!

I think I was made by an actor
I love the stage!

Joanna Hobbs (9) Broomwood Middle School

MY SISTER

My sister,
Feet are like cheese,
they scare away the fleas.
When she starts to cry,
her tears are like whisky milk.

She's thin and smells like a bin,
she just can't help eating cheese,
she's always pleased by eating it.

Was she made in a cheese factory?
I don't know.
But I know she does not like snow,
I have to play alone,
and she always wants to sing a solo.
She loves to sing I'd love to beat her in,
But her feet keep me back.

Craig Reardon (10) Broomwood Middle School

11

L'ESCARGOT

The shell is a house.
A body like a slug.
A neck like a giraffe.
Antenna is like an eyelash.
Walks as fast as a turtle.
Slime like thick, runny water.
A shell like a legendary fossil.
Curled up like a cat.
It's a knight in shining armour.

Leanne Kershaw (10) Broomwood Middle School

MY MUM

My mum is a lamb,
soft and gentle,
like a summer breeze.
She works so hard,
like a ferocious sea!
Her eyes are so blue,
as bright as a sunny day!
Where would I be without
my mum?

Stacey Illingworth (10) Broomwood Middle School

THE CELLAR

I've never been down in my cellar
Never seen what might be down there,
Might be a big hairy gorilla
Or a zombie or a devil with hideous hair.
A tiger or a lion from London Zoo,
A troll that only comes out at two.
A vampire to suck lots and lots of my blood
A dragon with 8 heads or a swamp full of mud
Some blood sucking bats or a big grizzly bear.
Some slithery slugs a goblin with a horrible glare.
A tribe of ants on the run
A huge hairy man with a big rifle gun
A python, or a witch who will cast a spell
A gruesome demon that belongs in hell
A big hairy spider with little ones beside her
I wonder what's down in my cellar.

Romi Chantler (11) Brudenell Primary School

ALONE

I was sitting by the fireside
Alone
Everyone's gone out and left me at home
Alone
At school everyone's got friends but me
Alone.

I go home wondering why I'm lonely maybe
I'm bad or maybe I'm sad.
I get home it's all quiet I think all
Alone.

Riffat Siddique (11) Brudenell Primary School

THE CLARINET

Isn't it great
To play the clarinet
I don't know what it is
It's just the feeling you get.

I was feeling so brill
As I stood on the stage
I looked at the music
Turned over the page.

I heard that noise
That horrible squeak
I felt so low
I felt such a freak

I jumped off the stage
Ran as I cried
So worried they'd shout
So I ran fast, to hide

I ran to the shop
Bought some Polos
And that was the end
Of my clarinet solos.

Holly Prosho (10) Brudenell Primary School

KIDS HAVING FUN

Clash batter cram natter
kids having fun
mum shouts them once or twice
but still it's smack and punch
up and down round and round
kids having fun
mum shouts them once or thrice
but still it's crack and crunch
scream and yell scream and yell
kids having fun
mum shouts them once or more
and shouts them for their lunch.

Richard Ineson (10) Carlinghow J & I School

THE MAD COW

Four legs a body a head so big in a field talking to a pig.
The sun was shining in the sky and the cow was eating a blackberry pie.

The cow was walking in the field when it came across a duck that squealed
Then he went into a supermarket with his trolley and nowhere to park it.
When he saw a piece of beef he felt that he'd become a thief

Causing havoc in the shop he felt that he'd have a drink of pop
Then he felt very sleepy and supermarkets are very creepy

Then he returned to his field
His mother gave him a right big shield
Then she sent him to his room
There to await a fate of doom.

James Wilson (10) Carlinghow J & I School

WOOLA LOVE

My baby little Woola love,
All soft and fluffy ball of fluff.
He fights and scraps with the other cats,
But mostly on poor Malcolm's veggie patch.
My baby little Woola fluff,
He loves to lie around,
And when I give him a little stroke
He makes a purring sound.
When my little Woola love is
Hungry for a bite.
He drools and purrs around my
Legs with all his little might.
I love my little Woola fluff,
All soft and full of cuddles.
When his little pink nose runs,
He makes gooey little puddles.

Eleanor Summers (10) Carlinghow J & I School

SPRING

Birds are flying all day long.
Birds are singing their lovely song.
Spring is a lovely season.
You see buds, in the woods,
Tra la la laa laa laa!
Now the days are getting longer.
Now the flowers are growing stronger.
The air is full of pleasant smells,
Daffodils, daisies and bluebells.
Up on the moor you can see all the ling,
God has rung the bell of spring.

Frank Mayfield (8) Christ Church CE School, Pellon

SPRINGTIME

Springtime is a lovely time,
Plants are starting to grow and grow.
Out of the grass the buds peep,
Then the plants open up and show their lovely springtime look.
New life is here, new leaves, new green grass,
And new birds all around.

Oliver Boylan (8) Christ Church CE School, Pellon

WAITING FOR SUMMER

Waiting for summer is very long.
On cool nights we go on nature walks.
In school we have the summer games.
The summer fair too.
In the holidays we go down the wood
and feed the donkeys.
Nature's out on the cold summer nights.
Going on holidays are the best.
Flowers growing bigger each day.
On the top of the highest hill.
Rivers flowing with fish big and small.
Sometimes having water fights is fun.
Under the waterfalls we walk.
Mud had gone, grass had come.
Me and my cousins go for rides in the country
and see nature running free and wild.
Echoes on the other side of the rivers.
Rolling on the grassy hill in the summertime.

Elena Illingworth (8) Christ Church CE School, Pellon

WAITING FOR SUMMER

We are waiting for a lovely holiday
A lovely day to play out, play anything you want to
In summer there is lots to do
Thank you for coming back summer, we've had enough of winter
Nature you see in summer
Going on holidays
Football you could play
Or you play cricket
Racing, you could do in the summer
Sunshine you see shining all around
Umbrellas we don't need to use in the summer
My mum can sunbathe in the summer
My mum takes me to swimming baths in the summer
Everyone's waiting for summer
Raining you're not gonna see in summer.

Michael Farrer (8) Christ Church CE School, Pellon

WAITING FOR SUMMER

Welcome summer
All nice things you bring
I can't wait to go on holiday
The European games are nearly here
I like the fantastic weather
Nature hangs waiting for summer
Glory hangs around the corner

Foals are growing,
Open countryside all dry waiting for us.
Roaring wind and scorching sun.

Summer endless days
Umbrellas we do not need.
More beach mats, oh yes please
Massive weather improvements
Earwigs are back unfortunately
Rain is history.

Fenella J Bowling (8) Christ Church CE School, Pellon

TOWN AND COUNTRY

Quiet heather in the country,
Battered roads inside the town.
Tranquil moorland in the country,
Never seen inside the town.
Quiet evenings in the country,
Gorgeous sunsets in the town.
Horses silent in their fields,
Dogs lay silent in their kennels.
Till the springtime yearns again,
When the landscape is reborn,
Life begins in the country,
When the springing hare returns to live,
In the warrens which it digs.
The country is the life for me,
The town doesn't appeal to me.
Country is quiet, tranquil,
Town is busy, boisterous
Country is the very best,
The only place for me.

Christopher Davies (10) Cliffe Hill School

WINTER DAYS

It's dark when you come home from school,
Dark, dull days,
Feel warm inside as you think of home.

Mum makes hot, steaming apple pie for tea,
I snuggle up and watch TV,
Wrap up warm when you take Minnie the dog for a walk, says mum.

Don't want to get up in the morning,
I'm too warm and snug in my bed,
Outside the ground is frosty and crisp.

You can see your breath as you walk to school,
Huddle up in your coat at playtime to keep warm,
Wish you hadn't forgotten your gloves.

Time to think about Christmas,
About what presents I would like,
Hip horray! Snow is falling outside.

It's the weekend before Christmas,
And the snow is very thick,
I enjoy having snowball fights with my friends.

The Christmas tree is up,
Amy, mum calls, come and help me make mince pies,
Yummy, yummy, they are scrummy!

Happy Christmas, Amy, said mum on Christmas Day,
I open my presents, one by one,
It's going to be a wonderful day!

Amy Lea (10) Cliffe Hill School

THE BEAUTIFUL COUNTRYSIDE

The beautiful countryside,
Its fields and forests are filled with trees
And sweet smelling flowers smell beautiful,
Lakes, and waterfalls splash in the sun.

Wildlife dances around
In the long shiny meadows
Where the grass, and trees sparkle with gleam.
Horses gallop and run through the
Sun, and the gentle breeze.

If you listen carefully you can
Hear the faint sound of the tractor on the
Faraway farm,
And the stream rushing down very fast.

Children run and dance and laugh,
Running through the meadows and
Climbing up the mountains,
The sun starts to go down and
The trees whisper a gentle breeze.

Laura McMahon (10) Cliffe Hill School

AT MY NANNA'S

When I go to my nanna's
I always use my manners.
Because she buys me toys,
The sort that are for boys.
Like cars and trains and aeroplanes
And sweets and other special treats.
She even makes us dinner,
My nanna is a winner.

Ben Bracewell (9) Colden Primary School

21

THE MOON

The moon is shining on the tree.
The moon is shining with my friends.
The moon is shining with the stars.
The moon is playing tricks on me.
The moon is bright and light.
The moon is hot and shiny.
And the moon is shining gold and silver.
The owls are flying in the sky.
And the birds are sleeping.

Terilea Elder (7) Colden Primary School

NIGHT AND DAY

The deer pants for water,
The bees buzz in the grass,
The children are having a picnic,
The wasps are in the glass,
The trees give way to the light.
The badger comes out at dark,
Somewhere in the trees,
I hear a fox bark.
The cockerel crows at morning,
The badger is asleep,
And I cannot yet hear the baa of a sheep,
The cows are in the field,
And I'm eating an apple I've peeled.
Now it's dark the fox will bark,
The badger is hibernating in his set,
But I will never forget.

Sarah Lund (8) Colden Primary School

CAT BEGAN

She took the sparkle,
of the stars,
She took the greenness
of the emerald
And made her eyes
For her coat
she took the golden
of the sand
She took the softness
of the snow
She makes it shiny and smooth
She took the screeching
of the owl
She took the howling
of the wolf
And made her voice
For her walk
She took the swiftness
of the wind
She took the fastness
of the cheetah
And took the slowness
of the snail
She took the whiteness
of the moon
And made her whiskers
For her tail
She took the shaking
of a rattlesnake tail.
And a cat was made.

Gabrielle Brunning (8) Colden Primary School

THE COLD

The cold comes creeping up
the stairs.
And climbs into my underwear.

It starts to creep up my
toes,
Up my legs and in my clothes.

When I'm growing in the night
The cold creeps in and
gives me a fright.

I get up in the morning
To find that I am sniffing
and snarling.

Fay Garratt (9) Colden Primary School

THE ZOO

I went to the zoo.
But the monkeys had the flu.
The lions were too old.
The bears had a cold.
The elephants were big.
And so was the pig.
The mice were quite sweet.
The birds went tweet.
The camels had a hump.
The kangaroos had a lump.
The snakes went hiss.
And so did miss.
She said it was time to go.
But we all said,
No, no, no.

Lizzie Benn (7) Colden Primary School

24

THE KESTREL

The claws that grip,
The wings that fly,
The kestrel called
Its sober cry.
The evening is gone
And it is the night,
The kestrel is pausing
Before his long flight.
The rabbit sitting in the field
Is a very likely prey,
The kestrel hovers high above,
The rabbit has a price to pay.
The kestrel swoops down
On the prey unwary,
The rabbit is calm,
The night is still scary.
The rabbit squeals,
The grass just sighs,
The kestrel is the greatest,
He is the king of the skies.
Morning comes,
The kestrel is not here,
He does not like daylight,
For daylight is his fear.

Alice Jones (8) Colden Primary School

WHALES

Why couldn't you leave them alone,
They didn't do anything to you,
They're beautiful mammals,
They would be wondering what they'd done to you,
Thinking of an answer could not be done,
Day after day,
You'd do it again,
Being so proud of yourself,
For what you did,
Soon there will be no more,
Whales for you to endanger,
So please don't do it again.

Danielle Jenner (10) Cookridge Primary School

SPACE

Here we are floating in space,
Above the planet of the human race.

In our rocket the galaxy we explore
Avoiding the giant meteor.

Looking at the stars and low
Where shall we now decide to go.

We explored a planet called Mars
Which we found dodging between the stars.

No life we found it out to be
No animal, trees nor life could we see.

So we all decided to travel to earth
From which was our place of birth.

Philip Messenger (10) Cookridge Primary School

WHITBY POEM

Sea splashing
Sea rumbling
Screams screams
of a noisy beach
The wind howling
and trees
Scratching
A calm peaceful
harbour
Boats swaying against
the rocks
Children clapping clicking
with joy
as the sea begins to
settle
settle
settle.

Rachael Gibson (10) Cookridge Primary School

THE HAUNTED HOUSE

I see your firm dusty coat.
Your howl can be heard from a thousand miles.
Your windows swing open and shut,
Again, again, again.
You stand there all night long,
In the morning you're gone.
Waiting in the wings,
Next night, next night, you're
back!

Naomi Smithson (8) Cookridge Primary School

THE HAUNTED HOUSE

You stand there with jaws open, doors
slamming howls and screams.
Screech, screech, screech.
Where are your deafening noises coming
from downstairs, upstairs, where?
Where?
Windows open, freezing air clashing
through,
Who is in your wide open doors?
Your howls I hear so loud I'm scared.
The wind blowing in and out of your
windows and doors.
The night gets calmer the voice of
your howls gets deeper, quieter, softly
howling through my ears.
I'm wishing I could explore you,
I'm standing there. Then I run and
run and run.

Danielle Byars (9) Cookridge Primary School

WHEN I WAS VERY YOUNG

When I was very young,
Unlike eighty years of age,
I got a lot of work done,
Whereas now I'm trapped in a cage.

But when I was very young,
I had no grandchildren Daniel and Jane,
Then I knew nothing but could run,
Now I have knowledge and pain.

Joseph Taylor (9) Cookridge Primary School

WHITBY SEA

First the waves are still and silent,
in the ocean sea,
the next minute they are violent,
we must let it be.
First you hear a crashing,
then you hear a bashing,
a thunder storm will start,
then suddenly you start to feel blood pumping from your heart.
When the waves have once died down,
the wind will start to frown,
once again the sea is lapping,
because the waves died down.

James Horsley (10) Cookridge Primary School

BATTLE OF THE NOISES

Mars rising with extreme anger,
roaring with gusto, shaking the planets
like bombs hitting.
Making bangs like guns.
Erupting with sizzling steam.
Firing blows of wind.
Hurtling around as a fighter plane.
Jupiter strolling into main event.
Playing as an orchestra singing with tune.
Venus singing a beautiful song.
Sounding like a violin with a sweet song
so joyful.

James Neilson (10) Cookridge Primary School

THE WHITBY MOORS

Behind the heather on the Whitby moors,
is a beautiful grouse doing its chores,
See the birds soft brown and red feathers,
and see all the colours of beautiful heathers.
Just over the hill lambs waiting to be born,
have to wait until the breaking of dawn.
Their mother chewing on heather so sweet,
all the other sheep waiting for her to bleat.
Suddenly out pops the lamb of her dreams,
oh how elegant that little lamb seems.

Rebekah Dryden (10) Cookridge Primary School

RAIN

Rain comes down, pitter patter,
Where it falls it does not matter.
Down it comes, drip drap drop.
Nothing at all will make it stop.
It falls on the ground it falls down the drains.
That's what happens when it rains.
When it rains everything is wet.
That is what you must not forget.
When it rains everything goes.
But where rain comes from nobody knows.
Rain can be happy, rain can be sad.
When it's stormy, rain can be mad.
Rain comes down so, so fast.
But then it stops, it stops at last.
When rain's gone, everything's quiet.
Not like rain which is a total riot.
Without rain everything is calm.
But even so, rain's a total charm.

Kirsty Garland (8) Cookridge Primary School

ALONE

The boy is lonely,
The boy is sad,
Because he's lost
His mum and dad.

The boy's alone
In the great big house,
His rat has gone
So has his mouse.

He gets up and goes
To the dining room
To find his parents in the gloom.

He goes to the garden
And looks around
He sees his mouse
And then he cries.

My mouse!
My parents!
They're safe inside,
I'm not alone they haven't died!

Michael Smith (8) Cookridge Primary School

WHITBY

Whitby is a fishing town.
Ships and boats go sailing in and out.
See an abbey perched upon a hill.
The cliffs are beautiful no doubt about it.

Watch the waves roar and go back.
See all the ships in a big fleet.
Seals bob up and down on the sea.
Seals feed on fish like a treat.

Sometimes Whitby is very cold.
Freezing everyone as they flee.
Dracula moans near his grave.
Sometimes it even scares me.

Whitby was wet and windy when I went.
In Whitby I never saw the sun.
It was also very cold and chilly.
I always saw rain clouds it was never fun.

See the whale bones on the cliff.
They represent something very old.
A ban on whaling that is what it is.
Some very sad stories have been told.

Alec Taylor (10) Cookridge Primary School

WHITBY

The coach has turned I can see the sea.
By the abbey there is a lonely tree.
Look into the field and you'd see a pony,
Now night has come I feel dozy.

See some fish.
Let's make a wish.
My hotel's swish.
I like that dish.

I like reading my book.
It's about Captain Cook.
Oh no it's spitting just our luck.
In the museum I see a duck.

If you stand on a cliff.
You'd be lucky to see a ship.
There is no fee to see the sea.
So come along and splash with me.

The rocks are slippery, slimy and wet.
You shall be lucky to find loose jet.
People at Whitby very kind.
People at Whitby are merry and kind.

Helen Horsfall (9) Cookridge Primary School

WHITBY!

Lifeboats go out
For ships in distress
They never turn about
They might come one man less.

Dracula comes out at night
He drinks your blood
He can give you a fright
Then he might fall with a thud.

Some shells sound like the sea
Stones can shine because of the water
Then your face is full of glee
Some stones could be covered with mortar.

Whitby in a way is fun
It is in a National Park
Somewhere you might find some clay
On the wood there might be marks.

I've walked along the pier
There is a lookout post
Things seem a little queer
It is definitely on the coast.

Stefan Wagner (9) Cookridge Primary School

AGE

I am old too old,
I don't know my age.
Too old not bold!
I can't read the page.

I am like a lump.
I am slow not fast.
Too much like a hump.
I was fast in the past.

I can't believe I'm old.
I'm so old I'm late.
I am so so cold.
Now I feel like bait.

I feel so left out.
I am late and slow.
I am not known about.
I am so so so low.

I am too old to dance.
I am too too old.
I feel old with other people.

I am old too old.
I don't know my age.
Too old not bold!
I can't read the page.

Linzi Tate (8) Cookridge Primary School

WHITBY POEM

You walk along the pier
    The waves splash against
        the rocks
While animals of
    the sea
Sleep deep down on the
    sand,
Captain Cook stands boldly
    up,
While the whalebones lean
    against each other
Children paddle in
    the sea
While adults sunbathe
    upon the
        sand
Until the sun peacefully
    goes down
When night time comes
    The day is done.

Jade Nowland (10) Cookridge Primary School

WISHES

I wish I were a flower petal
floating high o'er vales and seas,
swirling, twirling, dancing,
prancing among the summer's breeze,
tangling, twisting, clinging,
yes clinging around the
tall withered trees.

I'd sail, sail with waterlilies
through and through
the peaceful lakes,
I'd hop through water plants,
and slither through tall green grass
like a snake.
I'd dance in the wind with
the fairies,
thank God,
and all this for nature's sake.

I'd fly over pink horizons
with flocks and flocks of birds,
I'd run and prance and
run and prance
with the deer in their herds.

Yes, my friend, if I were a petal
I'd float peacefully
eternally.

Emma Mason (11) Deanfield J & I School

AFTERNOON BREAK

Hayley plays with the hoop,
Hannah falls from the bars,
Vicky's doing cartwheels,
Jason's playing with cars.

Melissa's being a superstar,
Steven's teasing Nick,
Josie's gone to the toilet,
Max is tickling Rick.

The kids in class one are playing with bricks,
Lucy's playing mums and dads,
Daniel's fallen out with Sean,
Sarah's kissing all the lads.

Robert's running round,
Lee's fallen and cut his knee,
Lindsay's drawing pictures,
and I want my tea.

Playtime's nearly over,
so is the day,
I'm really tired,
from this play.

Rachel Jarvis (11) Eastburn J & I School

THE BULLY HE IS

On Monday, he waited at the bus stop,
fear appeared and so did a police cop.

On Tuesday afternoon, he called me names,
anger came and I got the blame.

On Wednesday he had a very good laugh,
and he followed me all the way up the path.

On Thursday we played games and had a shower,
then he bullied me with all his power.

On Friday, was the worst of all,
and he said, he shouted, fall girl fall.

Saturday's here at last,
I will try to forget most of the past.

Josie Atkins (11) Eastburn J & I School

THE MILKMAN

He starts work at 7,
He finishes at 10,
He does it every morning,
Again and again, he acts very jolly
Driving his float or trolley, he doesn't grumble
He doesn't fumble
But watches they don't tumble.
He starts work at 7,
He finishes at 10,
He does it every morning
Again and again.

Christopher Collier (10) Eastburn J & I School

PEACE AT LAST

On Friday there's peace at last
but soon the bullies will come back.

On Monday that was a dreadful day
because people kept calling me names.

Tuesday was very hard
because they were saying stuff about my dad.

Wednesday was the day we went swimming
they ducked my head under for a minute.

Thursday was no better
as they chucked muck at my sweater.

On Friday we had sport at noon
and they called me a big baboon.

Peace at last when I get home
least I won't get bored.

Gavin Wild (11) Eastburn J & I School

THE GANG OF BULLIES

Home at last,
I find it hard to forget the week that has passed,
Monday morning walked into school they all stand staring,
is it something I'm wearing?

Tuesday morning, is today going to be such a
dreading day,
should they still get their own way.

Wednesday morning was all right,
until I lost myself a fight.

Thursday morning was a school trip,
they made it seem like I was a drip.

Friday only seven and a half hours left at school,
I feel as though I have no power,
why do I feel so sour?

Charlotte Turner (11) Eastburn J & I School

SPRING'S WILDLIFE

Dawn in the woods
there are some holes
Animals live in them
not all are moles.

There's a village nearby
but the animals don't mind
The trees are thick
and animals are kind.

Animals go hunting
they sometimes bark
Then they come home
they hunt at dark.

Animals are around
so spring is here
if you see a hedgehog
do not fear
then you know spring is here.

Gavin Fairbairn (10) Eastburn J & I School

HOLIDAY INJECTIONS

Oh no!
It's the day for the doc's.
Do I have to go?

Look if you want to go on holiday,
Just have it.
He pulled out a syringe,
And just put it in a bit.

I screamed and shouted,
For about a minute,
He said 'It's over now'
I went and he binned it.

Oh no!
Tomorrow's the dentist's.

Hannah Woollacott (11) Eastburn J & I School

THE ANIMAL HOUSE

The garden gate gets stuck
Sometimes.
When it opens it's a squeaky mouse.
Down the alligator path
To the zebra door
Brown, blotchy giraffe walls.
With big shiny eyes as windows
Elephant coloured roof on top
Makes my house,
Noisy, crowded and friendly.

Adiel Hussain (11) Frizinghall Middle School

JUNGLE HOUSE

As I crawl down the jungle of trellis
       on this house,
I tried to be as creepy and as quiet
       as a mouse.
I see lots of scary slimy slithering
       little bits
That scare me utterly totally truly
       out of my wits
I feel a spiky set of antlers
that glisten in the moonlight.
Near the antlers I see a stubby
block of bricks that is open from the top,
and puffs out smoke like a dragon who's
just sneezed.
I slide down purple pieces of slate
like big elephant's flappy ears.
A long black snake slithers down, its
scales slippery and smooth,
glistening as the magical moon
       shines bright,
leaving all the animals in the jungle
       dazzled by the light.
A strong long door with a handle like
       Rudolph's nose
This place is absolutely brilliant,
       I suppose
Wow! I've made it from top right
       down to the bottom
This adventure has been totally
       really awesome!

Shataj Khan (11) Frizinghall Middle School

THE SECRET SONG

Who saw the leaf fall from the tree?
I, said, the rabbit, all alone.
Who saw the snow cover the mountains?
I, said the blackbird, but nobody knows.
Who saw the mice chew a nut?
I, said the dog, but nobody heard.
Who saw the plant grow?
I, said the bee, just me.
Who saw the cat kill a mouse?
I, said the caterpillar, the only one.
Who saw the rabbit bite a carrot?
I, said the worm, just the one.
Who saw the night star shine?
I, said the badger, just the mighty one.
Who saw the moon shine?
I, said the star, all by myself.
Who saw the seaweed grow?
I, said the fish, just the one.

Saqab Choudry (10) Frizinghall Middle School

THE SECRET ANIMALS

Who saw the petals grow from the rose?
I, said the bumble bee, only me,

Who saw the bricks break from the building?
I, said the spider, all alone,

Who saw the ship zoom by?
I, said the person, just me;

Who saw the icicles being made like sharp knives?
I, said the snow rabbit, only me.

Who saw the long green grass grow in the farm?
I, said the lamb, all alone,

Who saw the full moon shining like a light?
I, said the night owl, only me,

Who saw the mouse zoom into his hole?
I, said the cat, just me.

Tuseif Arshad (10) Frizinghall Middle School

SHINY HOUSE

There it is shining light.
Glistening through the dark
Cold night.
And a door that is
Varnished and keeps out
Cold.

A pipe that slithers up
Like a snake.
Over bright brown shiny
Stones.
That is when they're wet
Of course.
What a house!
All nice and shiny.
And my house is a
Sanctuary.

Shabana Hanif (11) Frizinghall Middle School

MY HOUSE

I am outside my house I can see,
The slimy slaty roof and sandy brick
Wall,
The shiny black pipe
And the new French windows
In the wall.
The wooden door window in the middle
I am going up the grey concrete path
But it is cold out
It is warm in the house
I had a thought, it might be cold
In my house
I saw a chink of light
I opened the door
There to greet me
Was the warmth of my house.

Wakas Arshad (11) Frizinghall Middle School

MY HOUSE

The gate to the garden is always open.
The path leads straight to the door -
Warm brown and welcoming.
The walls of sandy-brown bricks sparkle in the sun.
A huge living room window,
My mum cleans it every day
So it looks brand-new.
When the bedroom windows are open
The curtains flap about
As though they are waving.

The shiny grey slates sit on top of
The big oblong attic window of my bedroom
When visitors come to our house, they say,
'Your house is very clean and nice, we like it.'
So do I.

Rukhsana Aci (11) Frizinghall Middle School

TO WHOEVER GETS THIS MESSAGE

To,
Whoever gets this message
Please will you stop trying
to get me so you can show off
and so you can make me do
things like acrobatics and tricks
I am fed up with submarines
exploring my home
I am fed up with photographers
trying to take my picture
I am fed up with people trying to film me too
nobody would like it if I came
out of Loch Ness and started
to take pictures of you
or driving to your house
There is only one way you can help me
besides leaving me alone and that
is by being helpful and finding out if
I have got any brothers and sisters
in the world because I am very lonely
   From
     Nessie

Darren Cook (11) Greenwood Primary School

THE MOON

If you look up at the moon
for a long time
you will see a face emerge.
Stare and stare for longer
still you will see a whole new world
what would it be like
to walk on the moon?
All sandy like the sunny beach?
Dark like a room with no light?
What is the moon? I ask myself
Time and time again.
A lump of cheese?
A giant asteroid?
What is the moon?
I want to know.

Lyndsey Ashton (10) Greetland J&I School

AUTUMN AND WINTER

Snow falls slowly down,
On my mum's face comes a frown.
All the fields are covered with snow,
All the flowers cannot grow.

Nobody can play about,
Nobody can play, sing or shout.
All the beauty from summer has gone,
Surely all this is wrong.

Everywhere is so peaceful,
Beautiful sledges, reindeer pull.
Christmas day is very near,
Santa Claus will soon be here.

Tracey Mollet (9) Greetland J&I School

NIGHTSHADE

Galloping, galloping through the woods,
hear the sound of thuds, thuds, thuds.
Horses here, horses there, horses
nearly everywhere.

I jumped on Nightshade and off she ran,
through the bushes and on to land.
I stopped to take a look around,
and found myself in a crowd
a crowd of bushes a crowd of trees,
a crowd of all different scenes.

I started to canter on my horse,
and flew through a running course
I got a trophy for winning the race,
and I had a happy cheerful face.

Samantha Perry (9) Greetland J&I School

FEAR

Fear is black,
It tastes like red hot blood and
smells like burning coke.
It looks like a ferocious tiger from
hell and sounds like a fearful
beating heart.
Fear feels like death is approaching.

James Quigley (10) Greetland J&I School

WHAT IS . . . THE MOON?

The moon is a sparkling diamond,
resting on a black velvet cushion,

It is a blob of vanilla ice-cream,
in a river of chocolate sauce,

It is a white swan,
sailing on a lake at night,

It is the cream,
floating on a cup of cappuccino,

It is a firework,
illuminating the night sky,

It's like a golden nugget,
resting on a bed of ash.

Stacey Nunns (10) Great & Little Preston Junior School

SPRING

Spring is here
The flowers bloom
The day is fresh and bright
I look upon the field's edge
What a pretty sight
A pretty bunch of daffodils
Swaying in the breeze
But the grass has just been cut today
And all I can do is . . . *sneeze!*

Zoe Orme (11) Great & Little Preston Junior School

KIRSTY AND THE MISSING RING

Kirsty did a silly thing
She went and lost her diamond ring
She looked outside
She looked upstairs
She went to look at her friend Clare's
Kirsty could not find it there
She ran and sat upon a chair.

Kirsty ran to the bathroom door
She looked all over the slippery floor
She could not find a single thing
No sight of her beloved ring

Kirsty started singing
And flinging her arms around
Her mum sees her from the door
And yells, 'You silly singer!
Your diamond ring is on your *finger!*'

Amy Robertson (10) Great & Little Preston Junior School

KILLING ITS PREY

Silent creeping towards the rat
As quietly as a midnight bat
Rustling of leaves on the ground
The snake's body slithering around
His beady eyes watch the prey
Snap it's gone at the last light of day
There he goes into the grass
No-one knows where he did pass.

Vicky Norman (11) Great & Little Preston Junior School

COLOURS ARE THE WORLD

Colours are the world,
The sun and rain.
The trees in autumn,
The leaves they need to gain.

Colours are the world,
The sea and sky.
The snow in winter,
That melts and I say goodbye.

Colours are the world,
The animals and bushes.
The ponds and forests,
Where there are fish and thrushes.

Charlotte Pitchers (11) Great & Little Preston Junior School

SNOWFLAKES

Whirling twirling in the air,
Dancing all around,
Snowflakes flying everywhere,
Some hitting the frosty ground.

Twisting swirling in the sky,
Moving all around,
Lace dots high as high,
Spinning upside down.

Snow is getting slower and slower,
Stopping all around,
When I awake the next day,
Slush is on the ground.

Shelly Norman (11) Great & Little Preston Junior School

WHEN MY BROTHER'S EATING JELLY!

When my brother's eating jelly,
He gets it everywhere,
He dribbles down his chin,
He drops it on his chair!

He gets it round his mouth,
On his jumper too,
He drips it on his face,
All this is very true!

He flicks it on my skirt
He throws it at my hair,
He catapults it in the air,
It flies off *everywhere!*

It trickles down the door,
It splodges on the floor,
And when his bowl is empty,
He yells and screams for more.

And then . . .

When my brother's eating jelly,
He gets . . .

Emma Wilson (10) Great & Little Preston Junior School

WINTER

Whizzing whirling in the night sky,
as another snowflake falls as it hits
my window pane,
I can almost feel it touch.

The snow starts to sparkle
outside my bedroom window,
then the snow starts again falling
silently,
covering all the things in sight.

Cold and wet
the snow is set
almost like a quilt of jewels.

The snow falls again,
when it hits the quilt of jewels
the blanket sinks to the floor.

When I woke up the garden is cold wet
and green,
the sun has not left a sign of winter,
oooo! No the snow has gone.

Jenna Byram (11) Great & Little Preston Junior School

ARE WE NEARLY THERE YET?

Are we nearly there yet?
The kids all shout
We'd only been
Round a roundabout.

Are we nearly there yet?
The kids all cry
Sophie's been sick and
Adam's squashed a fly.

Are we nearly there yet?
The kids all wail
David got mad and
Pushed Sally into Dale

Are we nearly there yet?
The kids all scream
Holly hits Peter
Then spilled his ice-cream.

When we got there
We had a look around
We even saw a little fox
Being chased by foxhounds.

On our way back
All I heard was
Are we nearly there yet
Again and again and again.

Katie Brownridge (10) Great & Little Preston Junior School

BATTLE OF THE SUN

The sun begins to rise,
Into the sea blue skies.
The ground is lit in wonder.
And then, a crash of thunder.
Dark clouds dominate the air.
Spreading dullness everywhere.
The sun peeks through a cloud.
And then a mighty sound.
The dark fights back in rage.
It's like a giant cage.
Trapping all the light.
So it may win the fight.
The sun breaks free into space
And sends the dark to another place.
The air is calm and full of light.
But it is drawing near to night.
The sun sets in the rainbow sky.
The colours catch everyone's eye
The sun's gone down for another night.

Paul Mitchell (11) Great & Little Preston Junior School

THEY HAVE FEELINGS TOO

I went to the zoo the other day,
But what I saw left me in dismay.
I thought the animals would be roaming around,
Instead, they all lay there bored on the ground.

They were all locked and bolted in cages,
It looked like they had been starving for ages.
I wanted to cry, but I couldn't protest,
For I was much smaller than all of the rest.

I think that all animals should be free,
But I don't think that anyone would listen to me.
You think it's amusing to see bears dance and sing,
But you never really thought how the bear is feeling.

Did you!

Claire Fletcher (9) Hinchliffe Mill J&I School

I KNOW THAT THERE IS SNOW!

The sky is full of brightness,
The land is full of whiteness.
Although I am in bed,
With the pillow over my head.
I know,
That there is snow!
Reaching up are glistening trees,
On the ground are icy leaves,
Because of the wintry, freezing
feeling,
And the coughing, sniffing, sneezing,
feeling.
The curling up and wheezing feeling,
I know,
That there is snow!

Ginny Louise Whiteley (9) Hinchliffe Mill J&I School

SNOW AND ICE

The snow looks like a sheet of white with icy
specks on its face.
Walls and classroom roofs are white as white
can be.
There are footprints with filigree
round the edge.
Icicles with sparkling shiny sides
and the points look sharp and spiky.
A biting bitterly freezing cold wind
is hitting my face like a boxer.
I see swirling winds blowing
snow around. Like a tornado far
above the ground.
Then I go home and to bed and dream of ice and
snow and cold winds that blow.

Robbie Woodhead (10) Hinchliffe Mill J&I School

THE WIND

It roars like a bear
As it blows through our hair
And the dust and leaves, hit our legs and knees
It steals your washing
While you're not watching
And quickly blows itself away in a breeze.

Rachel Goodyear (8) Holy Name Primary School

SNOW

Cold is the snow as it daintily falls
Stripping the trees bare from their leaves
Falling on rooftops making them white
Covering the world with a soft coat of white.
Cold is the snow as it madly falls
Landing on doorsteps blocking up doors
Then we wait for another time it falls.

Laura Harvey (9) Holy Name Primary School

WIND

Round and round the world I go
Making the leaves swirl as I travel
Tearing the trees free from their leaves
Banging on the window rattling at the door.
Banging and crashing like it's never done before
Whipping round the houses
Flapping at the washing hanging from the line
Banging and crashing making people whine.

Roseanne Dowe (8) Holy Name Primary School

BRUSH YOUR TEETH

Brush your teeth,
Every day,
If you don't they'll rot away.

Brush them in the morning,
Brush them at night,
Keep on brushing them,
Keep them white.

Mums will nag,
Dads will scream,
I'll be brushing my teeth,
In my dream.

Rachel Lyons (10) Hopton Junior, Infant & Nursery School

ANIMALS

They can be big,
They can be small,
What ever size they are I love
them all.
They can be fat,
They can be thin,
I don't care if they live in a bin.
They can be wet,
They can be dry,
Some can live up very high.
Birds in a tree,
Mice on the ground,
They're all animals that can be
found.

Melanie Brooke (9) Hopton Junior, Infant & Nursery School

BLOOMIN' TEACHERS

Bloomin' teachers,
You know what they're like,
Stand you in the corner,
Keep you in all night.

Pick on you for silly little things:
Swearing, shouting, mis-sing-out-full-stops,
Joining up cap-it-als to the other letters,
Sneaking down to the corner shop.

When you say 'It was her as well!'
The only reply to pass teacher's lips:
'I don't care about her,
It's *you* I am talking to!'

He says that I'm stupid and my work is scruffy.
He's a cunning foe.
But he's never answered me this though:
What was he like as a boy?

Now this is the end of my poem,
I cannot write any more,
If teacher sees what I've written,
My head will be part of the door!

Luke Wilson (10) Hopton Junior, Infant & Nursery School

COME ON YOU REDS!

All of a sudden the crowd are on their feet
Cantona is on the score sheet.
By half-time the score is 1-0
Newcastle fans feeling ill.
I relieve my shoe of some dirt
And peg it at a Newcastle shirt.
Second half things are getting worse
Ferdinand is on the burst.
United are still going strong
It appears they can do nothing wrong.
Final whistle the reds go top
To the dismay of the Newcastle crop.

James Laycock (11) Hothfield Street Junior School

ROALD DAHL

I like Roald Dahl,
He was a good writer,
I like his stories,
They keep getting better.

I like Fantastic Mr Fox,
I like the BFG,
I also like Esio Trot,
They all have a very good plot.

Roald Dahl was good,
Roald Dahl was ace,
He was the best story writer
Of all times.

Helen Rishworth (11) Hothfield Street Junior School

GHOSTS

I believe in ghosts,
I get quite scared,
I believe in spirits and ghouls
But I don't have nightmares!

I don't like ghost stories,
Although they're not true
I believe in coming back from
The dead
On Friday the 13th I stay in bed!

I don't like old pictures
Of people who are dead
I don't believe in God,
Even though he rose from the dead.

Full moons freak me out,
Horror films look so real,
But ghosts just spook me out,
And sometimes I just have to
Shout!

Emily Needham (10) Hothfield Street Junior School

MY CAT

My cat is black and white
She hardly ever bites
Her name is Minstrel
She likes to play with tinsel
Her age is seventeen
But that age she doesn't seem
Sometimes she's sick
But only a little bit.
      I love my cat.

Peter Gunn (11) Hothfield Street Junior School

ASHLEY

He's helpful, he's furry, he's my little boy,
He has a little time to play with a toy,
A misty eye, not good enough no more,
Is blocked by splittering darkness,
A gleam in his eye,
I hope he'll never die,
That's my boy Ashley,
His eyes are mine,
But mine are not his,
If he ever dies, I'll call my next one Liz.
I'll always be blind,
No matter what,
That's Ashley my little boy.

Joanne McLoughlin (10) Hothfield Street Junior School

TENNIS

Strolling in,
Crowd going wild,
Feeling confident,
Lots of pride!
The game starts,
I serve the ball,
Great, she missed it,
I whack it back.
Points to me!
Points to me!
Yes! I win, I walk up to get my trophy,
Crowd went mad screaming, cheering.

Michelle Starmer (11) Hothfield Street Junior School

HORSE RIDING

Long hard day
Seemed like years.
I'll never forget,
Horse riding.
It's my big day, for,
My riding competition.
I put Pearl's saddle on,
I put Pearl's reins on,
I put my hat on,
I got my whip
And I was ready.
I started to practice,
I told Pearl to jump,
It was so high,
I thought I was flying.
Pearl was excellent,
She didn't need practice.

Carla Pearson (11) Hothfield Street Junior School

A SUMMER DAY

When daylight dawns and sun comes
up.
Birds are singing, flying high
Like a concert in the sky
Flowers open petals
Looking towards the sun
Children together and having fun
When the day is done
Children go home
Until another day.

Suzanne Cuthbert (11) Hothfield Street Junior School

HOCKEY MANIA

Smacking the ball to another player,
The rain crashing on the vicious floor.
Snow violently coming down
The ball was on fire.
Whack the ball went with speed
A crash of lightning came
My body shivered with fear
Crinkled fingers.
My mind was frozen
The other side smashed the ball into the net.
When would this day be over
Rain came down harder
Splash, splish,
Puddles surrounded my feet
My legs wouldn't move
I was soaked to the bone.
My face was pale and white
I'm in agony playing in such ferocious weather
We gawped at each other in pain
This game is driving me insane.

Lisa Meehan (11) Hothfield Street Junior School

WITCHES AND WIZARDS

Witches wizards *ghosts* and ghouls,
Can spook us all to look like fools.
They make you *shiver* and make you shake
They make your knees begin to quake.
In the darkness of the night they make
You see an awful sight.
Shadows stretch in weird wild ways.
Make us long for bright safe days.

Dawn Wigglesworth (10) Hothfield Street Junior School

MY SILENT CAT

He sat by the door
Sneaked in,
Jumped up,
Curled up,
Fell asleep,
He purred a lot,
Got up,
Chased his tail
Couldn't catch it,
So went back to sleep,
Woke up,
Started to scratch,
I shouted,
He looked up,
Knew he had got told off,
He walked away.

Fiona Bowden (9) Hothfield Street Junior School

SAM

Sam is my dog,
He sleeps like a log,
Lying so quiet and still,
His coat is so white,
His eyes shiny bright,
His nose is so black, wet and cold,
And when he starts barking,
At people who are parking,
You know he sounds ever so bold.

Laura Clark (11) Hothfield Street Junior School

MY CLASS

My class has broke the window glass
I hope I pass my spelling test,
But still, I like my class.
Our class has flowers everywhere
Paper or real it doesn't really matter,
Their petals peel off all over the place
But still my class is ace.
Our class has made a Henry VIII he's
Nearly as tall as the ceiling, if you
Came in the class tonight
The sight of him would give you a fright
Our class has talked about the weather
We did an assembly to Mrs Feather
We looked at rain, sun and ice
And still my class is nice.
Our class gets the answers.
Each week we do our tables test
Because Mrs Leech likes maths the best
But if you look north, south, east and west
You will find our class is the *best*.

Rachel Wallbank (9) Hothfield Street Junior School

WHAT I HATE WHAT I LOVE

What I love about rugby is
scoring over the line.

What I hate about rugby is never
getting the ball.

What I love about rugby is rolling
in the mud.

What I hate about rugby is when you
get hurt.

What I love about rugby
is smacking the ball over the
post.

What I hate about rugby
is the ball isn't shaped right.

What I love about rugby
is pushing in the scrum.

What I hate about rugby
is getting really cold.

Ben Cartledge (10) Hothfield Street Junior School

THE ANGRY DOG

He was lonely,
His family had gone to the
Cinema.
He went to the tissue box.
Ferociously he destroyed the tissues.
He got so angry.
So hungry.
He charged into the door.
Bang!
His head bumped into the door.
Eventually he got through the door.
Into the kitchen.
Straight to the bread bin.
A whole packet of bread
Rustle, rustle, and rustle really
Loud.
He gave a big loud . . .
Woof!
He wasn't hungry any more.

Laura Whitely Smith (10) Hothfield Street Junior School

SIZZLE AND DRIZZLE

Sizzling drizzling
Rain or shine, the weather might rain
The weather might shine.
Fish, fish
Like the rain
Pitter patter on the rooftops
Then the sun shines bright and clear
And the rooftops
Dry quick
And slick.
The rain starts to drizzle
While the sun is out
Now look in the sky
Look at those colours
Bright and clear in a semi circle shape,
That is called a rainbow
I heard my mind murmur.
Then I remembered the colours of the rainbow
I remember the song we sang
So I repeated it over and over again,
Richard of York gained battle in vain,
Richard of York gained battle in vain.

Amber Louise Smale (8) Hothfield Street Junior School

DRAWN ACROSS THE STRINGS

You're taken out of your comfortable case
When you see something shiny
Which looks like a ring.
But of course it's only a shiny
Violin string. Heck ooo stop stop
I can't take any more!
Day by day it's getting better
No more squeaking and no more strangled
Cats.
It's like you've suddenly been hit
With a bat!
Heck ooo stop stop
I can't take any more!
Being a bow is hard work!

Rebecca Steeples (9) Hothfield Street Junior School

MY PUPPY

My puppy chews everything in sight
And she cries in the night.
She is a real brat
She even chews my best hat!
Sometimes she howls
But on the other hand she sometimes growls!
My puppy likes butterflies
But she can't get at them because they can
Fly!
I like my puppy
She is great
And she licks our plates
My puppy has black fur
She does quite the opposite to a purr!

Jack Weeden (8) Hothfield Street Junior School

RUNNING

Running fast
Running slow
All the best
To win the show.
People young
People old
Run outside, when it is cold.
Some people like
To run for fun
Ready steady hear the gun.
Run at night
When it's not light
Wear a vest
To make you bright.
I run with my mate Ben
Oh watch out for that car.

Luke Arrowsmith (8) Hothfield Street Junior School

MY ANGRY SISTER

My angry sister
Stamps her feet
Screams
Punches everyone in sight
Then says *You're really mean*
Pulls faces, sticks out her tongue
Never gives up till she's won
You've guessed it
She's won.

Jenny Ross (10) Hothfield Street Junior School

CAT CAT

Cat cat
in the night
glowing hard
glowing bright
tapping
on the letter box
scratching
on the door
climbing in a cardboard
box
Cat cat
in the night
glowing hard
glowing bright
falling falling to
sleep zzz.

Katie Harrison (10) Hothfield Street Junior School

WHAT EVER NEXT?

I saw a buzzy bumble bee being taken for a walk,
I saw a cold cup of coffee that couldn't keep still,
I saw a big furry cat play to itself,
I saw a collie dog being sold,
I saw an old wooden table wash its coat,
I saw a new keyboard waiting to be drunk,
I saw an old tatty pigeon that stung me,
I saw a block of empty flats at the fair,
I saw a bouncing kangaroo in the city,
I saw my usually quiet headmistress on the roof!

Lucy Peel (10) Hothfield Street Junior School

UNDER THE BED

'Ted Ted,
Clean under your bed.
There's a crisp packet
And ear wax and all such
Things as that.
Ted Ted clean under your
Bed,
Before I clip your ear.
Look it's wet
Here have you been drinking
Beer?
There's bits of fluff,
And junk and stuff,
I don't know what to
Do
Tidy up this mess
I can't take any more.
It'd better be spick and
Span,
Before it gets to four.'

Simon Heath (9) Hothfield Street Junior School

74

RUN UP!

Pouring rain,
Soaking wet,
Running faster,
Win the bet.
Go go go goes the crowd,
They do really make me proud.
Getting louder *go go go*,
I'm not never gonna slow,
Got the ball,
Run run run
This is really having fun.
Nearly there,
At the line.
Now the weather's turning fine.
Chant, chant *go go go!*
Sliding try,
Have scored,
Look at the ref,
Look at the crowd,
Silence like it was vowed.
Then it broke with joy and screams.
Now all the faces have gleams and beams.

Jenny Tate (11) Hothfield Street Junior School

TRAMPOLINING

Trampolining is so fun,
You can go twirling whirling round
and round
Before you know it you're upside
down!
Your hair tosses up and down
The springs are going round and
round
If you wear rings they're bound
to fly off
So please, please, please take them off
You are bouncing up and down
At the end of the day
You can go this way, that way
anyway you want.
Most people go twirling, whirling,
turning, boinging and somersaulting.
Oh No! Someone's coming
That means I will have to stop
trampolining and get off
Then I did a somersault
and off.

Nicola Robinson (9) Hothfield Street Junior School

TENNIS BALL INCIDENT

Tennis ball over the wall
Go and get it, I'm not.
Where is my ball?
Over the wall, but where?
Up in the tree
Under the tree,
In the flowers.
You shouldn't have hit it with so much power.
There, it's in the flower bed,
But, can I get it?
Maybe I can,
Maybe I can't, but I'll try.
What if I break the plants
I creep to the flowers hoping she doesn't see me
What if she sees me she'll be mad for the rest of her life
What shall I do?
I'll get it.
So I crept to the ball
Hoping I didn't break the plants
Luckily I didn't
I got the ball and ran
I was glad that was the end of that
I never played tennis again in my garden.

Leanne Wainwright (11) Hothfield Street Junior School

DO POLAR BEARS?

Do polar bears eat pears?
Have they ever tried them?
Do they growl?
Do they bark?
Are they very smart?
How can they survive in the snow?
How much do they know?
Do they dig a den?
Or do they live in a pen?
Do they swim in lakes?
Or slither like a snake?
Do they eat butterflies?
Or do they make mud pies?
Do they ride a bike?
Or do they catch a pike?
Do you think he will share it
With me
If I come for tea?

Gwen Needham (9) Hothfield Street Junior School

MY MOLE

I was digging in the garden
that very last Sunday
when a little snout popped out as
pink as pink can be.
Then a head and body as
black as black can be.

Then I realised it was a mole.
So I picked it up and named
it little mole.
Then put it in a hutch
and fed it far too much.
So then he was as fat as can
be!

Jemima Olivia Robinson (9) Keighley Preparatory School

MY KITTEN

My kitten is just a ball of fur
He's dark brown, light no-one can
decide.
I think he is just so cute I do not
really care.
His eyes are blue, as big as the moon
and stars.
When he is in a room of light
there is a twinkle in his eyes
but he is just so cute I do not
really care.
His tail is so bushy it is very nice.
My friends say that is the best
bit of him but I do not think
so,
but he is just so cute I do not
really care.

Johanna Weston (9) Keighley Preparatory School

GORDALE BECK

White water bubbling
Flowing over mossy rocks,
Sparkling in the sunlight
Crystal clear
The whooshes of the water quite near,
Children talking, children splashing.

Rachael Kirby (10) Kingsway Primary School

GORDALE BECK

Glistening Water,
Over rocks it flows,
Really rocky river bed.
Darting currents,
All along the stream.
Looking at the scenery behind it,
Ending in the sea.

Bending, turning, twisting, squirming like a snake,
Ever going onwards.
Crystal clear,
Knocking on the side of the rocks.

Gemma Walton (10) Kingsway Primary School

MALHAM'S RUSHING STREAM

Running rushing stream
Splashing and crashing
Against mossy rocks
Sun shining making the river sparkle,
Looks like drinking water,
Bits of foam here and there,
Birds cheeping,
Ahh . . . peace at last,
Almost silent
Shhhhh . . .
Splash! Splash! Splash!

Rachael Greaves (10) Kingsway Primary School

GORDALE BECK

Gordale Beck
Fast and quick
Tinkling like bells
Splashing like fish
Beautiful waterfalls
1000 different greens
Bubbling like it's full of bubble bath
Amazing scenery
So wild
Muddy, rocky river bed
Rustling trees
Stepping stones over the crystal clear
Water
Seeing your own reflection
Now that's what you call
Gordale Beck.

Simon Newton (10) Kingsway Primary School

SILENT WALKING

Breezes flowing through my hair.
Ships cruising to other docks.
Wind whistling in my ear.
Silent river ripples on the muddy bank.
Silent grass swaying side to side.
Seagulls pecking at the
Wriggling worms in the soft gooey mud.
Flowers dancing in the listening wind.
Trees hanging over the swishing river.
Ships break the silence and sound their sirens.
Birds flap their wings and fly away.
Dancing flowers close for tomorrow's day.

Jade Shaw (10) Kingsway Primary School

RUGBY

Run and pass
The ball
To a player
On my side
To score a try

On the field
You can feel
The tightness
In the scrum

A drop goal
Tension is on
To score a goal
Yes!

Jamie Greenway (10) Kingsway Primary School

FOOTBALL

Players run on
Crowds go wild
Roaring
Shouting
Screaming
Kick off
Ball flying
Through the air
Like a fireball
Skimming
The defender's head
Brings the attacker down
Penalty
Hope we score
What a goal!

Andrew Longfield (10) Kingsway Primary School

GORDALE BECK

Water falling
Dropping down
Rushing down stream
Water racing down river
Travelling really fast
Slowing down as it reaches the sea
Flowing over mossy rocks
Fish swimming very fast
Clear water rushing
Sparkling like glass.

Mark Holgate (11) Kingsway Primary School

GORDALE BECK

Blue stream bubbling
Mossy rocks slipping
Currents are shallow
Bubbling away like a washing
machine
Small waterfalls, splashing
Reflections on the stream
Water rippling
Crystal clear
Water flowing with speed over mossy
rocks
Grassy banks
Walking along bumpy paths
Starting to rain
Splish, splash splashing.

Jennifer Marston (11) Kingsway Primary School

GOOLE DOCKS

The boat is still,
The white swan is moving slowly on the water
The grass is fresh
Yellow flowers, old bricks.
Big boats in the background.
Crane as big as a dinosaur.

Leigh Clarkson (9) Kingsway Primary School

GORDALE BECK

Rushing water
Glittering like gems
Flowing over mossy rocks
Sparkling, shining in the sun
Children in the river, splash, splash,
Birds singing, 'cheep, cheep'
River flowing with speed
Making rocky river rapids.

Lindsay Martin (10) Kingsway Primary School

FARM ANIMALS

Cows, horses, pigs and sheep
All through the night they go to sleep
They wake up when the sun is out
Then the horses run about.

The farmer comes along some days
And they all run in different ways.

Lyndsey Farish (10) Kippax Greenfield Primary School

THE FUNNY BUNNY

My favourite animal is a bunny
She is very funny
She has a den in the shed
Where she makes her own
little bed.
On a morning she runs
round the garden hoppety
She likes to go to the shop at the
top.

Leanne Beever (10) Kippax Greenfield Primary School

THE CAR JOURNEY

Going down the Motorway
in your car
trucks at one side,
motorbikes at the other.

We turn off to a side road,
out pops a tractor, the brakes
on, with a little screech.

We carry on a little and we're
there at the campsite,
what a journey!

Richard Ratcliffe (10) Kippax Greenfield Primary School

THE FISHY TALE

Cool and calm as the deep blue sea
Seaweed swirling as fast as can be
Fish swimming slowly in a coral reef
Floating lightly like a leaf
Some are patterned, some are plain
Some are like little droplets of rain
There are some female fish and some male
And that's the end of the fishy tale.

Rebecca Lamb (10) Kippax Greenfield Primary School

THE WORLD OUT THERE

Stuck in this chair all day
Stuck in this room all day
Stuck in this house all day
No-one to play with
No-one to talk to
The world out there
The sun out there
The sky out there
The grass out there
The trees out there
Everything out there!
But me, stuck in here
In this room
In this house
Oh, how I wish someone would
come
How I wish I had some company
How lonely could anyone be?

Claire Mitchell (9) Larks Hill J & I School

BLIND LONELINESS

He sits
Hearing not seeing
He wishes he could see.

At the window he hears children
Shouting with glee
Wishing he has friends in his world.

Alone he sits
All alone
How he wishes.

Teresa Speakman (9) Larks Hill J & I School

THE FOX TRAP

The hunter had come and set some
deadly traps
The fox doesn't know what danger it leads
him in
The trap snaps shut and digs into the
flesh
The fox yelps with a face that is hurt
and eyes filled with pain
He lay there waiting, waiting to die as
the moon rises.

Stevie-Ann Harrison (9) Larks Hill J & I School

LONELINESS

Everything still, not moving
Nobody playing with each other
Just nasty people
Murder is always here
Not a friend to play with
Not a nice village at all
Me stuck in the street
Nothing to do
Everything still, not moving
Sound is lost
Lost somewhere
Friendships have gone forever.

Rebecca Walker (8) Larks Hill J & I School

ACROSS THE ROAD

I look across the street, I see it
the house across the road.
Surrounded by a heavy darkness
Oh how I wish she'd open her
curtains, they make the light
inside grow dim.
Sometimes I go and knock but
it is no use, she cannot hear.
I wish I could find the key to
unlock the sadness from her
mind.

Danielle Knee (9) Larks Hill J & I School

IS SOMEONE THERE?

My face is blank with a stare
There's no-one to talk to, no-one there.
I keep on thinking there's someone there.
But inside it's not fair
I wait and wait for a friend
But a friend is nowhere to be
found.

Amit Patel (9) Larks Hill J & I School

SNOW

Swirling, slowly
Gracefully, silently
Wait a minute
It's gaining speed
Racing rapidly,
Speeding swiftly
Battling in combat
Fighting it out,
To reach the cold freezing ground
Slowing to a standstill
The snow has stopped
Sparkling, shining
The sun comes out,
A child's paradise
Snowballs fly, sledges glide
But when night falls
Everything stops
And the cycle starts again.

Steven Barrow (10) Larks Hill J & I School

WHITE

I am white.
A colour that doesn't exist
everyone else is a colour
but I am the odd one out.
I am the one that doesn't belong
with everyone else.
I belong in my own set, the lonely set
but why should I have all the loneliness
and pain?
Why don't you feel what it is like
to be lonely?

James Shaw (9) Larks Hill J & I School

SNOW

Swirling and twisting through the air
On the roof tops, trees and hair
Battles and fighting are going on
Until night falls and it has gone

No more crystal flakes are falling on the ground
But the howling wind makes them dance around
The mist clears, the sun comes out
All is quiet and not a sound
Nothing is there - no-one is about.

Natalie Seddon (11) Larks Hill J & I School

MY MIND

Deep down into the darkness
feelings appear to be grey
and I hide my feelings
deep down inside.
The thing that hangs on is *anger.*

James Stott (8) Larks Hill J & I School

WINTER DAYS

I wake up
To a white world outside
Collect my sledge
And slide, slide, slide.

My nose turns red,
My lips turn sore,
My eyes are runny
My hands raw.

The snow flutters softly
Down on my face
Whilst me and my sledge
Go at such a pace.

The crystals swoop down
On every bare tree
On every object
Including me.

The sun comes out
No more snow
Nipped by winter
Time to go.

Robert Nowak (11) Larks Hill J & I School

OUT THERE

Out there, mum
and dad drive
into the black
night.
Out there, a
lonely owl
hoots.
Out there, a
silent robber creeps.
And there's me
in my bedroom.

Out there, the
wind whines.
Out there, the
trees shudder.
Out there, a
silent cry for
help.
And there's
me in my
bedroom.

Matthew Thrall (8) Larks Hill J & I School

SNOWFLAKES

The crisp white snowflakes whirl around
Swiftly and gently into the dark
Unknown.
Riding on the wind
Turning and dancing
Swooping down
Soon the sky is empty
Only a few little snowflakes ride
On the roaring wind
They twist and lift
Landing on the soft white carpet
Of snow.

Natalie Guy (10) Larks Hill J & I School

SNOW

Snowflakes swirling like feathers
from a swan
Gently floating down from
the dull dark sky
Landing softly on a plush
white carpet
With layer upon layer of
sparkling crystal flakes.

Faye Sidaway (11) Larks Hill J & I School

SNOW

The whirling pearls float softly down
Like an elegant dance from the sky
to the ground
They grow and lift
Swoop and dive
Now they are racing through the air
Swirling madly
Fighting fiercely to the ground
Slowly they settle down
They cover each roof of every house
And each twig of every bush
The sun is out
The snow has gone
No more racing and no more fun.

Jack Storr (11) Larks Hill J & I School

THE MYSTERIOUS DESIGN

Snowflakes float down silently
Fighting fiercely to the ground
Down they come, swaying and twisting
Elegantly they flutter and prance
Swirling and twisting as they go
Where they land nobody knows
The sun's blinding rays are here again
As the last crystal flakes fall down
The sun fights to gain its place
To discover what's under the mysterious design.

Ashley Hewes (11) Larks Hill J & I School

THE OIL SPILL

It was tragic to see the birds
And seals covered in oil
And them being taken to be wrapped
Up in cloth and put in boxes
And taken to an animal hospital.

Me and my friends feel guilty
That our oil rig was polluting the sea
And that the oil was killing animals
And that the money that we get
For the oil will go straight to help
Clear the oil in the sea and
To help the birds
And seals get well again.

Stephen Bryden (10) Lightcliffe C of E School

MY DAFFODIL

A meadow full of daffodils blowing in the
breeze. There's a lovely cream
petalled one with lovely
orange and yellow
pollen
My
lovely
daffodil
A
sun
shining
down
on
me.

Natalie Thorn (7) Lightcliffe C of E School

THE ROSE POEM

The little rose is
dancing in the sun.
Swaying softly gliding
in the wind. The flies
come darting, hovering
drifting through the
sky. Swallows, swans
crow around to watch
the rose sway
in the sun.

Maxine Harrop (11) Lightcliffe C of E School

WHAT IS RED?

Red is a rose shining bright
Standing tall in a garden
Red is a ruby
Sparkling in the light
Red means danger
A warning colour
Red is a fire engine
Speeding through the street
Red means stop
On a traffic light
Red is the blood
That comes out of your body
Red is embarrassment
Running off stage
Red is anger
Running round your head.

David Kemp (8) Lightcliffe C of E School

EASTCLIFFE

Wind blustering by,
Like the sound of grass rattling against each other
Seagulls drifting in the breeze
The sea letting out its scent
Mixing with the cool cold clean air.
The waves crashing down on the rocks
Looking down on the town the people are rushing about
Shopping and working.
Cars are beeping their horns
I feel cold and alone.

Matthew Broadbent (11) Lightcliffe C of E School

THE HUNTING POEM

I stood there watching from behind a tree
Watching the man with the big top hat
Watching the man with the big red coat
His grand gold buckles twinkling in the light.

I saw him saddle up his horse, he began to trot around
I saw him start to look around
I heard him when he called his hound
They circled the wood together
Until the hound let out a cry.

I saw them run after him
I heard the cry
I clenched my fist
I saw it running back again
I was relieved
But I knew a good huntsman never gives up
Without a battle.

Then with one almighty crash
I ran out from behind the tree
Only to find a little brown heap lying there.

I saw another, the huntsman ran
I felt a shiver go up my spine, I felt terrified
I knew if he caught it I would blame myself.

They did not catch it
The huntsman went red with rage and galloped
Deep into the wood
Why all the fuss over a baby fox?

Sarah Cadman (9) Lightcliffe C of E School

LORNA

She has hair like the saffron
rising sun
and eyes like the pale blue sky.
Her clothes so green they're
like forests stuck together.
Her hands so skinny like a
pigeons feet.
Her freckles are like orange splattered
all over her face
or maybe paint running down at a pace.
I wonder who this person is
can you guess?
Yes, it's Lorna.

Laurette Zarneh (9) Lightcliffe C of E School

LITTER BUG

Litter litter on the ground
City people looking around.

Rubbish, litter, pollution, trash
All of this from our cash.

Other people looking too
All of them wondering what to do.

Car fumes, oil, sewage, smoke
Making everybody choke.

So always put litter in the bin
Because if you don't
You will pollute the earth.

Amie Horne (10) Lightcliffe C of E School

THE PEOPLE IN POVERTY

I came to a place one day
It was a rubbish dump
In a town I think
What I saw was sad.

I saw some children
They were filling sacks
With a few tins
And some worn out clothes
They lived in cardboard boxes
What I saw was sad.

They didn't have a mum or dad
They didn't have any food
But we have
What I saw was sad.

They don't have a home to go to,
They don't have a warm bed
I felt sad when I walked away.

Daniel Seekings (10) Lightcliffe C of E School

MY MUM

Mags my mum is as pretty as a princess
her hair is as bushy as a squirrel's tail
lips as pink as peaches.
Her cheeks are as red as roses
And eyes as green as grass
She shouts like a bear when she's in a bad
mood
but she cares for me like a mother cat with
a new born kitten.

Laura Newby (10) Lightcliffe C of E School

MY FRIEND'S SISTER DIED

I came home from school one day
With something on my mind
My mother asked me what was wrong
There's tears in your eyes.
'My friend's sister died' I said
'That's why she was away.'
I got this letter from the teacher
She said to give it to you straight away
My mother opened the letter and read it to herself
Then she said to me,
'She wants us to go to the funeral
Tomorrow at half-past-two.'

So the next day I put my black dress on
My black shoes, coat and hat
We got to the church at a quarter-past
So we had a look around
At half-past the service started
It was all too much for me
They dropped the coffin in a hole
We said a prayer
Then I dropped to the floor
'She used to play with me, I said
I used to give her sweets
We used to play together every playtime
          But now she's gone.'

Chloe Leanne Cox (10) Lightcliffe C of E School

MY DAD

As gentle as a hamster
as clever as an owl,
He's bald but still he's handsome
and his eyesight's like a mole.

His heart is like a rose that is
just at the start of bloom,
His eyes are blue and sparkly
like a silver new cleaned spoon.

He's as happy as a hedgehog
that is safe across the road,
He eats just like a truck
ready for its load.

As short as the cut grass his
hair is a plain shiny brown.

His smile is like a bridge
except it's upside down.

Victoria Stobart (11) Lightcliffe C of E School

IF YOU DON'T GO TO GRANDMA'S

If you don't go to grandma's
You'll be grounded for a week
But mum, she calls me stupid names
Like sweetie pie and her dog's reek.

If you don't go to grandma's
You'll be grounded for a month
But mum, I don't want to
Go-Ya-little-runt.

If you don't go to grandma's
You'll be grounded for a year
But mum, she's so grumpy . . .
She really is a dear.

If you don't go to grandma's
You'll be grounded for your life
I feel sorry, for my dad,
With his noisy wife.

Suzanne McQueen (10) Lightcliffe C of E School

PUSSY

Black like the night time sky
Its whiskers long and bendy
Its teeth like the snow sparkling white
Its eyes green as grass.
They glow in the dark like a glow worm does
Its tail is long and black it curves and uncurves
It twists it around and points it up in the air
Its paws are soft and gentle but then its claws
Stick out of its paws and there not anymore.
Its nails are blazing white
Sharp like a knife
Its legs are strong, quite thin, but big enough to carry him
Places
Its body is quite big
Black, quite fat
Its furry and cuddly
Its ears are like bananas poky they stick up in the air
Sometimes they go back when it's cross
Its nose is squashed flat on its face like a
Pancake with two little black holes for its nostrils.

Elizabeth Johnson (10) Lightcliffe C of E School

IF YOU DON'T WEAR IT

If you don't have your party dress on by
the time I count to twenty, you won't go to the
cinema tomorrow.
I can't find it (thank god)
Two, it's on a coathanger in your wardrobe
I can't . . . found it. (Oh no)
3 get it on then 4
I want to wear my jeans
Five . . .
six . . .
OK I'll wear it I'll wear it
Seven remember your petticoat
Oh mum it's bad enough wearing *that* dress
nine, ten, eleven
I did it, I'm coming
Not those trainers you're wearing a dress! Twelve
Get off it mother
thirteen, fourteen it's mum to you.
OK mum
wear these . . .
But they're miles too small
15, 16, 17, 18
OK I'm dressed
19 do that hair
20
My lift's here
What lift?
Sarah, byeee
You're not going to the cinema
Tomorrow.

Natalie McCamley (10) Lightcliffe C of E School

BOURNVILLE

Eyes like deep black pools of oil with a brown ring
around the edge, the colour of roasted peanuts.
A nose like a wet sponge that's been soaked in
ice cold water.

A brain the size of a single piece of sawdust
Teeth as big as a sharks and a big mouth too
Claws as blunt as a butterknife
A tail that's powerful and strong with a
non-stop motor.

Fur like a sweeping brush walking around all
day long.
Ears like fluffy carpet dangling down from
his big head.

Mark Nowoslawski (10) Lightcliffe C of E School

COLOURS

Blue
Blue is a pool, deep and dark,
Always long and never ending,
Ever swirling round and round
Bubbling like a deep blue sea,
Cool and cold like ice in winter.

Red
Red is raging round and round
Red is anger, hot and bad
Steaming and smoking
Like fire in the night,
Burning flames so bright.

Rebecca Haigh (10) Lightcliffe C of E School

ON THE STREETS

We felt guilty because we ran away
We didn't have food or even a drink
We had to rummage in the rubbish bins
And we saw people looking upon us
People thought we smelt bad like pigs
We saw the people looking upon us as they got ready for school
The people who knew how to add and subtract
I wanted to wake up and be snug in bed
Why did it happen to us?

My little sister crawled along the ugly path
That lead to our cardboard box
We got stung by the nettles and how we cried
Branches poked us with their black fingers
We were scratched by the branches black ugly fingers
Why did it happen to us?

At last it was night a black frightening night
I could hear my sister crying
I felt like crying too
Slugs crawled along the ugly path
And some on our cardboard box
We could smell the dirty air of factories
And the smoke from chimneys
Why did it happen to us?

Emma Jane Robinson (9) Lightcliffe C of E School

WHEN THE EAST WIND BLOWS ON REMEMBRANCE SUNDAY

When the East wind blows on Remembrance Sunday
A hundred people's hair blows in its breath.
When the French horn blows, a hundred people's hats whip off
And are held over broken hearts as if to stop the grief
Pouring out.
Ladies and men weeping
Gold and silver medals clinking
Small children sleeping
When the East wind blows on Remembrance Sunday.

We all assembled on the rocky cliff and looked down
At the world so harsh.
Then looked up at the sky towards the distant heaven
Hoping to catch a glimpse of the loved ones that have passed
When the East wind blows on Remembrance Sunday.

Jimmy Smallwood (10) Lightcliffe C of E School

AN OLD FISHERMAN FROM THE SEA

Standing in a doorway in a leaning sort
of way, like the tilting of a boat.
A very big coat, a shabby old coat like the
rocks that have all been weathered.
His ears are big. He must always be able to
hear the sea, like the shells you put to your ear.

Two white sideburns which look like the foam from the sea.
Skin on his hands is very wrinkly patterns in the sand.
His fingers are thin like razor shells.
He is very aged like the cliffs that have been worn.
He is thinking, thinking about the life he has enjoyed on the sea.

Rebecca Riley (10) Lightcliffe C of E School

107

THE BULLIES

The bullies are waiting over there,
Where can you hide - where oh where?
You're meant to be their best friend
And now look where you're going to end.

If you ignore them they won't leave you alone
They speak to you in a horrible tone,
They boss you about,
And start to shout,
They call you names
And decide the games.

They act and look really cool
Even when they are at school
If I were you I would tell
Just after the teacher's rung the bell.

Sophie Bowyer (10) Lightcliffe C of E School

THE OLD FISHERMAN

His face is tanned and wrinkly
His nose is big and bent
His coat is ratty, his jumper's tatty
His hand is in his pocket
His hat is worn and wobbly.
His face is wrinkly too
His beard looks like the crackling waves
His wrinkly hand is holding a pipe and he is leaning against
a wall.
He looks very thoughtful
He's thinking about the past
About those times at sea with the waves crashing against the
side of the boat.

Grey Hawtin (10) Lightcliffe C of E School

ALL ABOUT MY FRIEND STEPHANIE

She smells as sweet as a flower
in a meadow, her hair blowing
around with the tint of sun
shining on it.

Her voice is quiet and soft
like a bird singing sweetly
in a tree. She has glowing
blue eyes that glitter and
sparkle as she looks around
herself.

She walks slowly and steady
like a snail on a good day
with her shell smooth.

Rachel Naylor (11) Lightcliffe C of E School

HOLIDAYS

I just *love* holidays
Away from school
Resting and relaxing
Whether it's hot or cold
Sometimes go abroad,
Sometimes stay home
Playing games or talking
To my friends by telephone!
When holidays are over
I'm overcome with dismay
Because shock horror! Woe is me!
It's back to school next day!

Alexis J Lea (11) Lightcliffe C of E School

COLOURS

Black is a black dog
chasing a black cat.
Black is the colour
of a smart bowler hat.

Green is the colour
of green, green grass,
that is in meadows
that sometimes we pass.

Yellow is the sun
during the day,
but orange joins it
as the sun melts away.

Red is the blood
in your veins.
Red is the colour
that stands for pains.

Robert Young (10) Lightcliffe C of E School

PEACE

Peace, love and friendship evermore.
Evil people we don't want in this world.
Agreement, let's settle things together.
Christ, the greatest peacemaker of them all.
Everlasting, that's what we hope peace will be.

Gareth Kitson (10) Lightcliffe C of E School

MONSTROUS TREE

Branches like arms
waving in the air.

Leaves stuck together like
the monster's scruffy hair.

Bark off the tree all rough
and so brown.

It looks like the monster's frightening
frown.

Eyes so big as red as
red berries.

His mouth is like a hole
in the tree.

And the flaming hot heat shooting
out of his mouth now that's
the monstrous tree.

Abigail Brooke (11) Lightcliffe C of E School

THE MONSTER

Waves crashing, damaging great mounds of rock
Which break off the cliffs, into the sea.
Birds scatter, while they can, to avoid the slipping rock.
All is changed, nothing will be the same again
As the monster creeps out, to conquer the world.

Thomas Harling (11) Lightcliffe C of E School

EMOTION

Empty inside, what should you do?
Motionless still. Stuck in a hole,
Options are not there, you can't get out.
Turn the key inside of me,
Inside I've managed, I can escape.
On the second the door will open,
No more sadness, I'm happy again.
I won't go back.

Mark Griffiths (11) Lightcliffe C of E School

MY BEST FRIEND'S FUNERAL

I went to her funeral
And stood right at the back
I couldn't live without her
I wanted to die.

Just two days ago
We were playing in the park,
I couldn't believe that she was gone
I just couldn't take it in.

I walked home slowly
With tears in my eyes
My brothers and sisters would laugh
If I went home crying
They didn't understand.

I went over the road
And into the park
I sat on a swing and remembered my friend.

I felt lonely and lost
Just sitting there,
All on my own
With nobody to talk to
Not even my best friend.

Sophie Angelica Thomas (10) Lightcliffe C of E School

THE BULLIED LITTLE VILLAGE GIRL

I am Jenny
The small little village
Girl
There I am standing in the corner
Surrounded with girls
As I stand there I cry
They say they're going to flush my
Head down the toilet
As other children come to join
They pick me up by the legs
And take me to the girl's toilet.
I am screaming and crying as
They put my head in the toilet
Then they flush the toilet
I am wet through
As they get me out I scream for help
But only one answered my call
They put me on the floor.

Tracy Wormald (11) Luddenden Dene J & I School

FIRST DAY

People said it would be great
It's a new school
But when I stood behind the gate
It didn't look so cool.

It's my first day
In the corner I stand
There's nowhere to go so there I stay
I've got no hope in the world.

114

A boy stands staring at me
I feel so small but then I see
He's walking straight my way
I've got no hope in the world.

He picks me up by the scruff of my neck
Then he throws me down
I did not know where to go
I just lay and cried.

Lucy Crane (11) Luddenden Dene J & I School

BULLIED

She had made no friends
She sat alone
Until Chay and her friends
Walked her way
She looked so scared
As they sat down beside her
'Go back where you came from'
One of the girls said.
Tears formed in her eyes
'We don't want your kind at our school'
Another girl said to her.
She stood and ran away
They called names after her
Then looked around the yard
For someone to torture
Just for fun.

Jodie Platt (11) Luddenden Dene J & I School

NOWHERE TO GO

I am at the park
all by myself
When all of a sudden
these boys come on

They slowly walk up to me
and shout
Get back to your own country
leave us alone

Why are you doing this
what have I done
I'm only here for a bit
and I've got nowhere to go

They're beating me up
punching and kicking me
Calling me names
I'm falling to the ground

They slowly drift away
I feel so small
Like a little lost boy
with nowhere to go.

Jenny Grant (11) Luddenden Dene J & I School

2 WAY BULLYING

I was on my way to the baths
When I saw Andrew doing his maths
So I went to him and kicked him in
Over fits of laughs.

He gets me in the playground with his mates
In the corner by the gates.
He calls me names and pokes fun
No-one to see, nowhere to run.

Now I've got him on his own
No mates with him, all alone.
So I went to him and beat him up
And after that he always shut up.

Chris Halstead (11) Luddenden Dene J & I School

WINTER

Winter is here it's frosty, cold
everybody cheers when
winter is here.
We like snow it's fun
snow flakes fall like
little raindrops
nothing grows not
even the crops
I put my foot in
my boot and I go
outside to play.

Rubina Ali (10) Manningham Middle School

WINTER

Freezing, shivering
from the cold, grown ups
don't like snow at all
when the wind blows
the children don't care
even if the trees are bare
I wear my hat
I wear my gloves
I put my cold shivering foot
in my warm woolly boot.

Asma Ullah (10) Manningham Middle School

HIDING TIGER

I am a hiding tiger keeping safe
I will not get out
I will never get out in my whole life
Then he thinks
But if I get out aggressive tigers might kill me
But if I get out elephants might feed me
But if I get out tigers might tickle me
But if I get out tigers might scare me
Then he stops thinking
And
I am a hiding tiger keeping safe
I will not get out
I will never get out in my whole life
Then he thinks
Why am I hiding is it my stupid brains?
Why am I hiding in the side of a zoo?
Is it because I am scared?
I don't want to get out!
Why should I get out anyway?

Affaan Mahmood (12) Manningham Middle School

WINTER

Now it's freezing
Fingers tingly and chilly
Icy cold like icicles
Streets covered in snow
People wearing woolly hats
Big boots to warm feet
Snow knee deep
Having snowball fights
People skidding and sledging
Skating on frozen lakes.

Faizul Islam (10) Manningham Middle School

SEASON POEM

Summer is nice and bright
Daffodils laying like bright light
The blossom colour is a lovely sight
I lay on the carpet of yellow light.

The lovely green trees
I dance in the meadow
With lovely summer dreams
The bees buzz hello.

The stars shine so bright
All the flowers around
The winds blow very light
Babies playing on the ground.

Hanna Hussain (11) Manningham Middle School

TIGER

She hunts madly
She runs like a flash
To feed her babies
When her fearful eyes,
Look in human's eyes,
And when she roars
For her lost cub,
She roars and her eyes burn like a
flash,
Her lost cub will once again come to
her,
She dreams about her lost cub
That she will find him and feed
him once more,
And years go by,
And now her cubs are Tigers
But she is still dreaming for her
Lost cub.

Shazad Razzaq (11) Manningham Middle School

TIGER POEM

I saw a tiger
In the middle of the night
He was a rough, tough tiger
With burning red eyes
He was hunting on his own
With his sharp teeth and claws
He was mean and keen, fearful
With burning red water eyes
If someone touches the cubs
The mean and keen tiger
Will be full of anger.

Asma Khatoon-Khan (11) Manningham Middle School

YELLOW

Yellow is the sun up in the
sky and fresh daffodils swaying
in the breeze.

Yellow is the taste of a sour
sharp lemon or the refreshing taste
of lemonade on a hot, hot day.

Yellow is the beak of a bird
chirping in a tree high above
your head.

Yellow is the feel of the hot
melting sun beating on my back.

Yellow is the smell of a spring
fresh morning or the smell of my
mum washing up.

Stacey Gibson (11) Mount St Mary's RC Primary School

FAIRGROUND FUN

I can hear the screaming echoing
And the sparkling lights crackling bright,
Everybody getting excited
Nagging to go on the rides
Babies moaning and groaning
Mums and dads getting bored , but are we? No!
Listen to the music around you
People yelling on the big rides
Look at the view on the big wheel
Listen to it crunch
People going home
All the noises fading away.

Steven Simmons (11) Mount St Mary's RC Primary School

UP IN THE ATTIC

A sudden bang from outside sends a
chill up my spine
The light from the trap door lets me
see a body on a stick
I hear screeching from in the yard,
Figures stand staring straight at me
A sudden bang makes me jump
I hope it was next door's old shed door
banging in the wind.

I hear howling as if a ghost was in
pain
I see eerie shadows upon the wall
There's creepy faces on the curtain
I hear creaking as if someone was
following me around the attic,
Ghostly shadows seem to watch me
wherever I go
I hate the dark.

Claire Dempsey (10) Mount St Mary's RC Primary School

CAGED UP TIGER

A caged up tiger, afraid alone.
No-one to talk to, caged up alone.
People just stare and turn away.
How can I live this way? I don't like
the food. I want to catch my own prey.
Talk to my own friends and have my
own way. But now I lay in a cage locked
up alone.

Christopher Barker (11) Mount St Mary's RC Primary School

FAIRGROUND AT NIGHT

Walking to the fairground on a
breezy autumn night
looking at the starlit sky

When you stand and listen
all you can hear is the laughter
of the adults and children in
the night

Blinding lights are all around
followed with the deafening screams
music playing soft from the horses
on the merry-go-round and a man
saying well done to a boy whose
just won.

Listen to the racket of the children
on the slide screaming while they're
playing on the winding ride.

Stella Kirbitson (11) Mount St Mary's RC Primary School

THE MIDNIGHT WAKING

I awoke to find perspiration soaked on my pillow
Gigantic clouds take shape outside.
A yellow fork drives down the grey gloomy skies.
My window gets washed from the lashings of pouring rain.
Another flash of lightening appears, a loud booming
Unexplainable sound bangs in my ears.
The whistling wind makes branches tap on my window.
Then my eyelids droop low, I start to get sleepy.
The next thing I know it is morning and the sun shines,
  The storm has gone.

Craig Asquith (11) Mount St Mary's RC Primary School

CAGED UP MONKEY

I am a monkey
and locked in jail
Nobody to care for me
No-one to talk to
Nowhere to swing free.
I'm never going to be free
as a monkey should be.

Sat in my cage with nothing to do
I am so lonely
I am so unhappy
I just want to be free
It is no fun locked up in a cage
I am never going to be free
to swing and sway
I'm never going to be free as a
monkey should be.

Joanne O'Neill (11) Mount St Mary's RC Primary School

THE ATTIC

In the attic just over there
funny sounds in the air.
Dripping taps, dripping away,
I'm frightened that's all I say.
Taps on the window, taps on the wall,
but the sounds from the attic
are the scariest of them all.

Shaking, shivering all alone
Sat under the attic on my own.
Bumps and bangs up there now,
what's up there? I'll find out somehow.
There's bats and rats and funny things
But the sounds are the scariest
that the attic brings.

Adam Trueman (11) Mount St Mary's RC Primary School

WINTER

Winter brings the chirping of
the robins and crackling balls
of snow. Children gracefully
laughing as they pull their
sledge on tow. I hear shots ringing
out from people hunting turkey.
I hear my feet splashing through
waters dull and murky. I see
the sparkling snow
clean and shining
The people wining and dining.
I see leaves that are dead
and crushed on the ground,
trees that are waiting for
spring to come round.
I see the glowing baubles on
a Christmas tree. I see the
glorious flames of a fire on a
winter's night, fighting off the
cold so we can all sleep tight.

Stephanie Carr (11) Mount St Mary's RC Primary School

BLACK

Black is a witch flying in the dark
night sky,
while her lucky black cat's left far behind.
Black is a blackbird rustling in a tree
and black is the bat who flies low above me.
Black is the cold night breeze that lies
all around.
Black is the badger walking across the
ground.
Black is the smoke coming from a fire
and black is liquorice that looks like
wire.
Black is tarmac freshly laid
and black is the remains of a blazing
warm fire.

Sara Hartley (11) Mount St Mary's RC Primary School

BETWEEN THE TREES

Down in the jungle between the trees
I hear strange noises amongst the breeze
The croaking of the frogs, as, they squelch
through the reeds.
The hissing of the snakes, as they slither
on their way, looking for their prey.
The giggling of the chimpanzee swinging
in the trees.
Squawk of parrots, as they fly away
last but not least, the growling of the
big cat wanting his feast.

Leah Plunkett (11) Mount St Mary's RC Primary School

DIFFERENT FACES

Loving faces kiss rosy cheeks
Rude faces call names and snigger
Sly faces act devious and crafty
While short faces try and stand
Up tall.
Complicated faces look puzzled
or hard
Hard faces stare and like
eating lard.
Careless faces trip and fall about,
While silly faces laugh
and shout.
Long faces droop and hang their
mouths,
And strong faces show off
flexing muscles
Sweet faces beam and look angelic
Small faces get lost in crowds.
And last but not least kind faces
look happy and proud.

Victoria Louise Broadbent (11) Mount St Mary's RC Primary School

THE SHINING SHIMMERING STREAM

I sat down on the dark green grass
Watching the shimmering stream
shining in the sunlight.
As I walk along the muddy bank,
I see rabbits peeping out of dark green grass
watching me as I walk alongside
the shining shimmering stream.

Nikki Rider (10) Mount St Mary's RC Primary School

MY SHADOW FRIEND AND ME

My shadow friend comes out
it woke me up.
We go and play in the street
where we meet our other friends
But me and my shadow friend
we dance and sing, nobody sees
us because they're asleep,
We have a party we played games.
When it is dawn and the
sun is coming up they
have to go away
but not for long they're back tonight.

Jenna Aylward (9) Mount St Mary's RC Primary School

BEHIND BARS

I'd like to be free
but not live in the sea
I would like to fly
in the blue sky.

I'm behind bars
a prisoner am I
It's not fair!
because I can't fly.

There's no food
I like!
I watch people play
on their bikes
It's not fair! It's not fair!
Being locked behind bars!

Laura Jayne Broadbent (9) Mount St Mary's RC Primary School

MIDNIGHT SHADOW

When midnight approaches
the shadow comes out
he looks around
to see what's about.

I heard a noise
what is that?
I thought it was Sheba
my beautiful cat.

Now it is one
it is past night
the shadow comes in
it gives a fright.

It's like a fight
it's like a show
Arrrgghhh he shouts
and off he goes.

Laura Pejovic (8) Mount St Mary's RC Primary School

THE SHADOWS

Shadows come out at night and
they give me a terrible fright.

I look out of my window and see
the shadows dancing out in the
street, Oh I wish I could go
outside and dance with them but
one thing mum and dad are downstairs.
Ah, I've got an idea, I'll climb out of the window.
I climbed out of the window, they all ran away,
I said, 'Don't run away please,'
they all came back,
we danced till morning.

Aimi Roberts (9) Mount St Mary's RC Primary School

THE HORRORS OF WAR

The desperate and injured people
Broken battered buildings
The shocking shattered people
Evil nasty Hitler
Bombing peoples houses
The sad and depressed people

Anger and rage from Hitler
The bloodshed over England
Children suffering from diseases
Homeless dirty people
The pitch-black nights going by
No food, people crying as the night
goes on.

Sabina Haroon (11) Parkinson Lane J & I School

THE VICIOUS ADOLPH HITLER

Children dying because of Hitler.
Children crying because there was no
food
Nasty Hitler strikes again
Trying to conquer the whole of Europe.
Carrying your gas mask because Hitler
sends no warnings.
Hitler sending doodlebugs because he
wanted to ruin our country.

Adnan Iqbal (10) Parkinson Lane J & I School

MY VISIONS OF THE WAR

The ruined buildings in the street
The desperate parents praying for
peace
The evil torture of the mind
The deadly silent night
The anguish building up inside
the heart
Adolph Hitler tearing you apart
The rubble lying in the street
The grey war that caused the grief
The deafening noises of the
bombs
The vicious people still carrying
on - and for what?
Their country, their lives, their
freedom and wives.

Sofia Butt (11) Parkinson Lane J & I School

THE HORRORS OF THE WAR

Horrible when Hitler dropped bombs
on the houses
Sadness when people lost their homes
Frightening when the war began
Evil soldiers that kill good people
Bombers dropped the bombs on the
factories
People starving for food dying of
hunger.
Little children when they lost their
father in the war.

Imran Mahmood (11) Parkinson Lane J & I School

HORRORS OF THE WAR

The black pitch of darkness
The evil, vicious, nasty Adolph Hitler
laughing away thinking that he shall
win.
The people worrying mad thinking that
they might die or become homeless or
even desolate.
The noise of bombs and guns firing and
exploding away
While the children who are suffering
and crying together hopelessly
People starving and crying for food.
All this happened because of Adolph Hitler.

Saima Tayab (10) Parkinson Lane J & I School

THE WAR

The bombs dropped
Everyone stopped
It was horrible
I felt miserable
Everybody worrying
I was hurrying to the shed
I saw people dying, also crying
I heard screaming from Mrs Minning
It's a vicious war and furious too
I sent a letter to my friend
He replied when will it end.

Nawaz Hussain (10) Parkinson Lane J & I School

SOUNDS OF WAR

Worrying all the time
Silence is all around
Deafening sounds begin
Hoping it would miss
Crashing and banging
Leaving buildings shattered and in
ruins
Hoping it would miss
Bloodshed all around
Miserable things to be seen
Everyone's feeling sad and unhappy
Refugees desperate to get away.

Afsha Ayub (11) Parkinson Lane J & I School

SPRING

Spring is here
The birds' songs are floating
in my ear
Their feathers are gliding
near my eyes
The scent of the flowers
shoot past my nose.
Animals are waking
bees are humming
Everything is here
we all cheer!
because Spring is *here*.

Zeennat Rahoof (11) Queen's Road J & I School

SPRINGTIME

Daffodils and tulips are opening out in spring
Blackbirds and thrushes are ready to sing
'Spring is here, spring is here
Let's get together and start the new
season of the year'
Caterpillars are hatching from the butterflies' eggs,
Trying their best to get out with their tiny legs
The birds have laid their eggs in the nest
The nestlings are hatching and having some rest
When you see the flowers open
and you hear the birds sing -
    Spring!

Sobia Jabeen (10) Queen's Road J & I School

FLOWERS MAKE ME HAPPY

When I feel sad
I look out of the window at the
bright, yellow and orange daffodils
and the purple white crocuses
looking at me
Whenever I look at the
beautiful flowers, a smile comes on
my face
I sometimes think to myself,
'I wish I was a daffodil or a crocus
and had those beautiful colours.'

Sameena Hussain (10) Queen's Road J & I School

HUNGER

When someone has nothing to eat
All they can hear is their heart beat.
When they go out in the street,
They have really weak feet.

When you go to bed you feel hungry
So you creep down to eat something
But your parents catch you and send you up
Then in the morning you eat a lot.

When you are hungry
You say, 'Mum, what's for tea?'
Your mum says, 'Bread and jam.'
But some people have ham.

When people have something to eat,
They can run in the street
With their strong feet
And they don't hear their heartbeat.

Zufran Ahmed (10) Queen's Road J & I School

WINTER IN OUR PLAYGROUND

One winter morning in our playground
The snow is falling heavily but there is
no sound.
People fastening their coats and tightening
their scarves,
Two girls cutting a hot cake in half
The children's scarves are being blown
away,
The snow has stopped the sky is grey
One girl throwing a snowball at her
brother.
The wind has stopped - the sun has
come out
People again throwing snowballs about
The bells ring, all the children
happily hum.
As they come in - a blackboard
full of sums.
Staring out of the window just
as the snow falls again.
There's a bit of hail and
a bit of rain.

Safia Hussain (11) Queen's Road J & I School

MONKEYS

Swinging from tree to tree
The monkey sweeps across the sky,
as long as you are high,
as long as the birds are flying,
so you can climb as high
as long as monkeys don't dare to die.

Marc Oldfield (9) St Giles J & I School, Pontefract

136

FLOWERS

Bluebells, cockle shells.
I'm going to tell your mother
for picking daffodils and at
night when the flowers are
all closed up, when the moon
came out fast and light shone
from the moon, it gave us a
fright, soon it was singing and
the sun shone upon them
and the flowers popped off their
petals. When they go pop they
are awake and they grow
beyond the day.

Jane Carter (9) St Giles J & I School, Pontefract

RAIN POEM

Rain is wet
And yet I know
Without the rain we couldn't grow
Grass or trees or have enough to eat
But rain . . . don't rain again
And keep me in the house
At play
I'd like to share the garden too.
The playground and the street
with you.
So come at night when I am
in bed
And let me see the sun instead.

Kelly Marie Aston (9) St Giles J & I School, Pontefract

137

JACK FROST

Look look! Jack Frost is there
How many icicles has he got there?
He will come in the night
and give us a fright.
In my house tonight
My fingers shiver my toes too
My body shivers like ice
all night.

Lindsay Livesley (8)) St Giles J & I School, Pontefract

IF I WAS A MILLIONAIRE

If I was a millionaire
I'd wear a golden crown in my hair
I'd have a throne, not a chair
I'd have a thousand teddy bears
I'd have a cinema
And a horse and carriage
So I didn't have to walk far
I'd live in a palace not a house
I'd have a pet mouse
I'd quit school
Buy a diamond jewel
I'd have a disco every night
With flashing lights so bright
I'd invite my friends to tea
They would bring a present for me
But all that is a dream
Or so it seems.

Katie Wagstaff (8) St Giles J & I School, Pontefract

A SCARY POEM

The sky is black and the moon is out
The street lights are on but
there's something about hiding, hiding in
the shadows.
Like a tiger fighting for food
Nobody go near it.
It's like a blood-thirsty hound
Oh no it's coming out from the shadows
It's a . . . It's a . . .
It's only a little kitten.

Daniel Thomas Miles (8) St Giles J & I School, Pontefract

MY VERY SPECIAL FRIEND

My friend is here
My friend is there
Every where I go
My friend is there.

When my friend is hurt
I am there for her.
When she's away I wonder
What she is doing. I think
About her and I wonder if she's
OK. I really miss her when she's
Away.

Me and my friend
Share things with
Each other and we
Forgive each other always
And that's why she is special to me.

Becky Stocks (9) St Giles J & I School, Pontefract

139

MY NANNA

I sometimes feel so hurt
to see my nana suffer.
Her eyesight going bad,
I feel so helpless,
just sitting there.
I get so worried,
with all the pills she takes.
I like to see her in the holidays
I sometimes help her in her
flat.
She makes me laugh when
she sings,
She has to have the telly on
loud.
Her hearing-aid bleeps when she's
on the phone,
I will miss her when she's
gone.

Karen Close (9) St Giles J & I School, Pontefract

MY FRIEND IS A GHOST

In the night he gives you a fright
he is white.
he sleeps in the day
he squiggles and wiggles
he's in my toy chest
he's in my vest
he opens the door
he falls on the floor.

I can't sleep
he acts like my brother
we play with each other
he is my friend ghost!

Sian Blackburn (9) St Giles J & I School, Pontefract

MY DOG

My dog is great
He is in fact my best mate
His hair is long and his eyes are brown
My dog is fun to have around
My dog's name is Brad
He is the best pet we've ever had
Brad plays a wicked game of football
Once or twice he has even managed to score
My dog is great
He is in fact my best mate.
Brad loves to walk and loves his food
And I think he is real cool dude.
My mum says Brad always barks a lot.
But he stops burglars taking everything we've got.
I love my dog and he loves me.
He is as good a friend as anyone can be.
My dog is great.
In fact he's my best mate . . .

Neil McCormick (10) St Giles J & I School, Pontefract

X-FILES

My favourite programme is the X-files
With FBI Mulder and Scully
Sometimes I wonder what it's all about,
And the enemy is such a bully?

The X-files is active and new
And always looks scary.
Mulder and Scully are so cool,
And always jumpy and darey.

Mulder is into UFO's and
Scully is so precise,
She's always neat and tidy and
That's what makes her so nice.

Karina Eustace (10) St Giles J & I School, Pontefract

TV

I like watching TV
It always makes me smile,
From Tom and Jerry's funny show,
To Road Runner running for miles.

My mum says that it spoils my brain,
Like scrambled egg on toast,
She shouts at me from the
Kitchen sink,
'You'll ruin your eyes you know.'

But what does she know
I ask myself? I love TV,
TV's my whole entire life,
And I think that it loves me!

Zöe Benson (9) St Giles J & I School, Pontefract

MY FAVOURITE COLOUR

My favourite colour is red
A nice red ball sitting on the lawn
A big red apple in the fruit bowl
A lovely red ruby in your ring
Santa's suit in the cupboard
A red stocking on the end,
of my bed.
      Oh how I love red.

Red is the sun when he goes
to bed
Red is my dad when he gets mad
Red is my packet of crisps waiting
Red is my pen rolling around
Red is a parrot squawking away
Red is the colour of my gloves
that I wear when it is cold
      Oh how I love red.

Jodie Whitaker (9) St Giles J & I School, Pontefract

FIRE

Fire here,
Fire there,
Fire running up the stair,
People dying while you're frying
In the world's open air.
The massive teeth,
It's colourful hands
The danger awakens with the devilish strands.

James Crashley (11) St John's RC J & I School, Normanton

CLOUDS

Clouds, clouds,
I like clouds
Wherever they are,
What ever they do
Whatever the weather
Pulling faces at you.
Big shapes, little shapes
Silver round the sides
Being very fluffy
Soft and white.

Big black clouds
Being very nasty
Making rain
And making thunder
In the plane
I feel
That I could touch the clouds
I've seen clouds close up.

Dominic Simpson (11) St John's RC J & I School, Normanton

YOUR HOLIDAYS

You get up early in the morning
tired and yawning, put your suitcases
in the car, then you know you've
to travel far, get to the airport
and depart, then arrive at your
favourite holiday resort.
When you've been and had
your cheer,
return back home until next year.

Dean McIntyre (11) St John's RC J & I School, Normanton

BIRDS

Birds gracefully glide by,
Birds fly high in the sky,
Birds fly low on the ground,
Birds fly round and round,
Birds twitter in the trees,
Their feathers sway in the gentle breeze.
The bird's feathers, nice and soft,
Suddenly the wind coughed,
Birds started, huddle together,
Everything shaking especially the Heather.
Blending with the lovely feathers,
The wind calmed down,
A feather floated to the ground.
A feather, fluffy, neat, petite
I was sorry to see the feather float by
High into the sky.

Alison Ward (11) St John's RC J & I School, Normanton

THE SEA

The blue green sea was rough and strong.
It has a bang and a clash of the waves.
Swaying from point to point.
How gloomy she does look.
In the dark misty night.
When the sea is dead and as calm as the death.
The sea is as cunning as a fox.
Its waves banging and crashing pebbles.
Fossils, rubbing against each other
I think the sea is calm when
the noise is less.

Bernadette McDonnell (11) St John's RC J & I School, Normanton

145

THE GIRL DOWN THE LANE

The girl down the lane,
Keeps herself to herself,
She's quiet, peaceful and shy,
She likes to wander, but talks
To no-one in sight.

She talks to the flowers,
She thinks they talk back,
People say she's mysterious,
But we know she's just shy.

She likes to sing,
But sings to herself,
Her voice is beautiful, sweet and high,
She sings to nature her glorious song.

She wanders day and night,
Past the butchers, bakers and florist,
She likes to wander by the park,
But never goes into play.

It seems as if she has no friends,
Should I be her friend?
Or should I not?
Perhaps she likes to be alone.

Sarah Kowalczyk (11) St John's RC J & I School, Normanton

THE NIGHT SKY

The moon stood proudly in the sky,
When a shooting star shouted near by,
'Get out of my way!' shouted the star
He zoomed near like a motor car.
'How can you be so rude?'
Shouted the moon, in a grumpy mood,
The star shot quickly by,
This all happened in the night sky.

'Twinkle, twinkle,' said the stars,
'I shine brighter than you!' said Mars,
'You don't shine brighter than me!' said Venus
'I bet you haven't even seen us,'
The moon yawned a big sigh,
This all happened in the night sky.

The moon was tired and ready to go
When suddenly the wind began to blow
The moon said, 'I'm tired and you're giving me a breeze,
The stars don't like you and neither do the trees.'
'It's tough,' said the wind, 'I'm not going away!'
'I like it here and I'm going to stay!'
This all happened in the night sky.

Kathryn Forrester (11) St John's RC J & I School, Normanton

SPIDERS

Most spiders are harmless
but some are not.
They can poison you or suck your
blood.
They can be as big as a
hand or as small as a pin.
Their legs can be furry and
really long,
or skinny and short
and very strong.
They're not really scary but,
they do look ugly when they
stare you out.
On their silky webs they wait,
to catch their prey and
store them away.
They wrap them up in thick
white cotton.
They bite off their heads,
or suck our their guts.
A spider's web sways in the wind and
glitters in the rain.
To flies a web looks like
heaven, but really it is
their doom.

Matthew McTigue (11) St John's RC J & I School, Normanton

148

THE MOON AND STARS

The moon is large high in the sky
It beams down making everything glow.
It looks very shiny but when you're up there
You'll know that it's made of rocks
And looks bare.
The twinkling stars that glitter and glow
That make a plough in the mid deep sky
It is as black as coal the midnight sky
The stars like little sharp lights
In a big dark room
They sparkle and twinkle
Until the night is done.

Anna Potocki (11) St John's RC J & I School, Normanton

THE WORST FEELING IN THE WORLD

The worst feeling in the world is when
You walk up to a shop and see
People queuing up to buy
The latest toy and you look in your pocket
To find
That you are a pound short
It's breathtaking
Heartbreaking
Brain bashing
To find out.

Owen Machen (9) St John The Evangelist RC Primary School, Bradford

THE TREE

They were coming through the forest
Walking, axe in hand!
Looking for the firewood that was in the land.
The tree could not run,
The tree could not move,
After a 100 years he was not so smooth,
He had once found the power to grow once again,
Then!
The evil executionists struck. Those terrible men.

Damian Yeadon (10) St John The Evangelist RC Primary School,
Bradford

ONE OF THESE DAYS

One of these days . . .
I'll show my brother who is boss
of each other.
I'll show him
that I'm not the weakest one,
I'll show him that I'm not his son.

He'll not be the one,
to send me up to bed,
he'll not be the one
to clout me round the head.
Yes!
One of these days
I'll show him who is
The boss!

Thomas Binns (10) St John The Evangelist RC Primary School, Bradford

THE DEATH TO THE TREE

The living grandfather tree, that was me!
Stood still, feeling the chill.
Autumn came and blew leavés away
Crashing and bashing,
The leaves tumble and crumble.
They sprayed a cross on me
They made me pay, for nothing!
They chopped my limbs with some violent things,
In shame and in pain,
I lived no more and I fell to the floor,
I was felled in half on the path
Because of that chain saw.
I died and am dead
I have ended up as a shed.

Andrew Lunan (10) St John The Evangelist RC Primary School,
Bradford

OUR SCHOOL IS A ZOO

The boys are monkeys, always climbing
trees,
And small children run around looking for
bees,
If someone's in a mood
They'll snap at you and be so rude
They are elephants always moaning
definitely roaring and always groaning
They are hippos always wetting
their faces
You also find them in different places
this school is full of animals in a cage
that scream and shout in noisy rage.

Nicola Bradbury (11) St John The Evangelist RC Primary School,
Bradford

DAFFODILS

As the break of dawn cracked,
as the birds sang sweetly,
I woke from my deep sleep
to the dim dark dull night.
I was sad, lonely and miserable.
In the morning
the golden sun glowed gloriously,
the green grass glittered resplendently,
everything seemed to be happy but me.
Hours of sadness, minutes of pain,
until out of the corner of my eye I
saw a daffodil.
My life changed.
The daffodil smiled at me.
Its golden trumpet shot out
of the pretty petals.
It winked at me and said 'Don't worry.'
Its green stem stretched strongly from
side to side with the sun's beam,
as though to say, be strong like me.
It danced with the wind,
it sang with the birds.
The daring daffodil changed my ways.

Lydia Jarockyj (11) St John The Evangelist RC Primary School,
Bradford

THE DAFFODILS OF THE NATION

Daffodils, daffodils, blazing they seem,
In spring they're anew, their glowing spires gleam.
Trumpets sweep their song of joy over the nation,
No dull colours, just green and yellow coloration.
Their flowing fashions always there,
Glorious, delicate, full of care.
They spread like a sea of rippling gold,
And when you pass you may pick one to hold.
They are dears, sweet and cheery,
They bring a smile to those who are weary.

Joanne Aveyard (10) St John The Evangelist RC Primary School,
Bradford

DEATH TO A TREE

There the tree stands, helpless and small,
He was the weakest of them all.
His long branch arms that reach up high
And his long thin trunk that points to the sky.
The other trees are bigger than him,
They're so strong and he's so thin.
Then one day as he stood in despair,
He could sense danger in the air.
It was man and their evil dragons
They charged at him in what were called wagons.
They came closer and closer until it was the end,
He was going to die and we would lose a friend.

Amy Donlon (10) St John The Evangelist RC Primary School,
Bradford

THE JOURNEY OF THE DAFFODIL

Today I look at you small and brown
My face begins to make a frown .
I plant you in the underground
and hear you make a cheering sound.

Now you know you're on your way
towards that sunny spring day.
When you unfold in all your glory
and join in with the Easter story.

How bright and outstanding you look!
So wonderful my breath away you took.
Your flower is like the golden sun
and brings a smile to everyone.

Why ever did I make that frown
I'll understand when you go back down.
No longer, I do need to frown and glower
because I've seen your shining crowning flower.

Julianne Doyle (10) St John The Evangelist RC Primary School,
Bradford

MURDER

One misty night it happened to you
A scream in the night
Blood and wood on the step.
The police came to take you.
They took you to the hospital
The doctor said you were stabbed with a knife,
They brought you here,
A graveyard in the country
And I'm here standing talking to you.

154

But there wasn't a scream in the night.
But a shudder!
It wasn't the police who took you away,
It was a truck!
And you were taken to a factory.
You were killed with a saw.
And I am not standing on a grave
But next to a piece of paper
That used to be a tree.

Michael Roberts (11) St John The Evangelist RC Primary School,
Bradford

THE TUDORS

Henry the VII, the first Tudor King,
Elizabeth the 1st was a popular thing,
But Henry the VIII was a greedy old fellow,
And Shakespeare wrote a play called Othello,
Edward the VI was crowned when he was
only nine,
And never would commit a crime.

First came Catherine of Arragon they say,
Then came Anne Boleyn with a chopped off
head and hey,
Here is Jane Seymour I know her too much,
Then Ann of Cleaves with her sensible touch,
Catherine Howard was beheaded alright,
But Catherine Parre was beautiful in sight.

And here I finish my poem at last,
The last time I do a poem about the past.

Sarah Bratley (10) St Joseph's RC School, Pontefract

SECRETS

Secrets, secrets, secrets everywhere
Whispering in the doorway, whispering on the stair,
The things people talk about in those hushed tones,
When they get spread what a lot of groans.

Such a lot of people trying to find out,
Trying to find out what the whisperings about,
Such a lot of people keeping them everywhere,
Best friends whisper whilst enemies stare.

Even best friends keeping secrets from each other,
Reminding you of you and your brother,
Such a lot of secrets cause big fights,
Some are so ridiculous they're about someone's tights.

Secrets are ridiculous, mad, crazy,
Some are about people being lazy,
Oh what a lot of secrets, secrets everywhere,
Whispering in the doorway, whispering on the stair.

Alice Parkinson (9) St Joseph's RC School, Pontefract

THE GARDEN GNOME

The garden gnome hides behind a tree,
The garden gnome wishes not to be seen,
Garden gnome thinks he's such a lark,
Garden gnome steps out when it's dark.

Little garden gnome blows on his pipe,
Little garden gnome gets such a fright,
Little garden gnome sees a human in sight,
Little garden gnome hides in the darkness of the night.

Little garden gnome hiding in a bush,
Little garden gnome sees a baby thrush,
Little garden gnome still as still can be,
Little garden gnome steps back behind a tree.

Patrick Jeffries (9) St Joseph's RC School, Pontefract

HENRY THE VIII

Henry the VIII
Ate and ate,
His six wives said,
'What a disgrace.'
Two were beheaded,
And one even died,
Two were divorced,
Only one survived.
His three little children,
Edward and Mary,
Elizabeth the first,
Who was very scary.
His place was big,
(Too big for this pig)
Hampton Court its name,
A great place for his game.
One of the six wives he had,
Haunts the place like mad,
So do some others,
That got lost in the night,
And they're the ones that give you,
        A Fright!

Tara Salter (10) St Joseph's RC School, Pontefract

THE KANGAROO

Once there was a kangaroo,
Who would not pay his bill.
For some strange reason,
He said he was ill.

I thought he was lying,
And wouldn't stop trying,
But he still refused.

Toad finally said,
I will go and see,
What is wrong,
I will find out.

Toad went to kangaroo's house,
Toad was shocked to see,
He was a louse.

Everybody now was,
Very, very sad,
Nobody knew he was,
That very bad.

They all called the doctor,
And he was soon here,
He said he's had too much beer.

Hayley N Duffy (10) St Joseph's RC School, Pontefract

158

THE CAVE

The cave, the cave
Let's start a cave rave,
Be careful if there's mud,
It's threatening to flood.

The caves are dry as a bone,
Scramble over the stone.
Slivering in the gloom,
Inside the mountain's tomb.

Underneath I wonder,
Above there might be thunder.
I can't hear the sound,
Because I'm underground.

The cave drips tears,
For one million years,
Then ever so slowly,
A stalactite appears.

Ahead there's a sound
Its waters were found,
The mountain has made,
A cheerful cascade.

The exit is found,
I'm up on the ground.
I turn off my lamp,
And go back to camp.

David Charnock (10) St Joseph's RC School, Pontefract

FIRE

Fire is a great phoenix,
With huge great wings
And gleaming, sparkling red feathers with a golden tail.
It rises into a enormous mass of fire
And screeches with a shrill voice
It beats its angry wings
And swoops over the wreckage at a speed faster than sound.

You can hear the crackling, sizzling sound as it walks,
And the smoky, roasty smell that rises from it in a fog.
It is fierce and fiery, raging and flaming
It rises and rises
And melts anything in its path
But after a while
It gets weary
And turns back into ashes.

Rebecca Roche (10) St Joseph's J & I School, Castleford

THE COUNTRYSIDE

The countryside, the countryside
With all its lovely flowers.
Crocuses purple, white, orange
Snowdrops white clean and bright
The trees green waving softly in
the breeze.

As I walk down the country path,
The birds fly high in the sky.
I can smell a perfume scent in
the fresh air in the countryside.

Tamsin Johnson (9) St Joseph's J & I School, Castleford

SPEED

Getting ready,
Don't be late,
Hurry up,
Won't want to wait.

Revving up,
Hear the noise,
Adrenalin flows,
Get ready boys.

Start your engines,
Round a bend,
Here we go,
Can see the end.

James Bird (8) St Joseph's J & I School, Castleford

RAIN

The sky turned grey,
the sun went in.
There it was shiny
and thin.
Dripping on windows
dripping on floors
falling off the gutter
splashing on the floor.
The sun crawls out
the rain goes in.

Breezy Wilson (10) St Joseph's J & I School, Castleford
.

WHAT IS THE UNIVERSE?

The moon is a torch,
shone under a quilt.
The sun is an orange wig,
laid on a pale blue shirt.
The stars are biscuit crumbs
tipped off a plate.
The earth is a swimming pool,
with Martians in it.
Jupiter is a planet,
which has too many spots.
Saturn is a finger
with a gold ring around it.
Mercury is a red bubbly,
which hasn't yet been eaten.
Venus is a green chalk,
stuck to a blackboard.
Pluto is an ice-cube,
out of the fridge.
Uranus is the neighbour,
of Neptune of course.

Thomas Morgan (10) St Joseph's J & I School, Castleford

FIRE

The fire is like a roaring lion trying to break free
He burns his way through everything but doesn't pay the fee
He spreads his big tail out and burns everything in sight
He is a glowing animal and glows so bright
He licks his way up anything that he can
And he is very dangerous to me, you and man
He is like a burning liquid destroying all the town
He is like a wild animal that will never be put down.

Siobhan Rudd (10) St Joseph's J & I School, Castleford

GET UP, GET UP

Get up, get up
you sleepy head.
My mother shouts
each morning
but I just like
to carry on snoring.
Your breakfast's out
it's getting cold
you're going to be late
brush your teeth
comb your hair
you're going to be late if you're
not there.
Get up, get up,
you sleepy head
my mother shouts
each morning.

Laura Grady (11) St Joseph's J & I School, Castleford

FIRE

Fire is a red squirrel
It darts across forests
Red and as hot as hell
Evil like the burns it gives you
Kept in a match
Impatiently waiting to strike again
Lightly, flashing, burning and melting
Like lightning it flashes and burns
Slowly it takes over everything it reaches.

Matthew Roche (10) St Joseph's J & I School, Castleford

163

I'M NOT AFRAID

When darkness falls noises I hear
Is any one out there?

The stairs creak I begin to shiver
Is any one out there?

Footsteps get louder and *Louder*
Please tell me is anyone out there?

A shadow casts upon the wall
I scream, is anyone out there?

A hand reaches out for the light switch
Oh, is anyone out there?

The switch goes down
It's only my mum who is out there!

Bernadette Kennedy (11) St Joseph's J & I School, Castleford

FLIGHT

Flying is like life,
Gliding through time,
The grace and freedom of flight,
Never ending.
Drifting on the changing current,
Soaring high and free,
Swooping down losing height,
The murky depths down below
Leaving sadness
Wreaks of pain.
Nature shows its anger with the rolling sea.

Robert Middleton (11) St Margaret's C of E School, Horsforth

FLIGHT

How I would love to be a kite,
I could fly so high and get away
I could escape, just fly away
Just fly and fly, fly like a bird
Up, up into the sky above
I would glide through the sky
I would cruise through the air
I would love to be a kite
Just fly away into the distance then
        Puff just disappear.

Holly Pemberton (10) St Margaret's C of E School, Horsforth

FLIGHT

Soaring through the air
Hoping to find adventure
Gazing down at the magical view below me
Amber wings swiftly move
Clouds dancing in the sky
Colour swings past my eyes
We gracefully move on
Flying on the big bird's back
Who knows if I'll ever come back?

Lynva Raworth (11) St Margaret's C of E School, Horsforth

FLIGHT

The bird drifts calmly, leaving the soft ground
Its body streamed with a mass of colour,
As it hovers, its outstretched wings flap silently,
Objects blur, disappearing to the naked eye,
It looks relaxed and elegant, quiet as a mouse,
Then it fades out of sight,
Its silhouette seen vaguely in the setting sun,
Never will I see it again.

Adam Baker (10) St Margaret's C of E School, Horsforth

SPLASH

My goldfish Splash swims around all day
He swims, he dives, he jumps,
It sometimes makes me wonder that he
doesn't fly out of his bowl.

He may not be very big but he is very bright in
colour.
His scales are orange and his fins are thin like
tissue.
Bubbles big, bubbles small this is how he talks to us
all.

People think he's not such a good pet but I've had
him a long time and he is.
       My Pet Goldfish Splash!

Gary Donoghue (9) St Peter's CE J & I School, Birstall

MY TEACHER

My teacher is really cool,
    she really is quite nice,
She helps me with my work,
    and calms me with my SATS.

She plays games with us,
    we play cat and mice.
She takes us on trips,
    and still she's really, really nice.

Kami Butterworth (11) Scout Road J & I School

SCOUT ROAD SCHOOL

Scout Road School
I like a lot
I think it's really cool
A happy place for me to be
So come along and you will see
The teachers here are really nice
And Joan's good dinner's worth the
price
The friends I've got I wouldn't swap
So Scout Road School comes out
on top.

Rachael Thorne (11) Scout Road J & I School

MY LITTLE CHICK

I couldn't believe what I could see,
When my little chick looked up at me,
I saw its beak just break the shell,
Then out it came so strong and well,
There it was all yellow and fluffy,
From that day on I called it *Plucky.*

Claire Thorne (11) Scout Road J & I School

EYE FOR AN EYE

Do back to them what they do
to you,
Shouting, punching and kicking too
What does it solve? What does
it prove?
It solves nothing at all, so make
the first move!

The world should be peaceful,
the world should be great,
it's harmony and peace not anger
and hate,
So be a friend and don't fall
out,
It's time to make peace and not
to shout.

Kathryn Louise Ingham (11) Scout Road J & I School

MY HOUSE

My room is always in a mess,
But isn't supposed to be,
So when I have someone to sleep,
I have to tidy up you see.

The bathroom is a smelly place,
I often go in there,
It's not that I like the smell,
But I have to wash my hair.

The living room is comfy,
With sofa, chair and TV,
I once watched David Attenborough,
And wished he was talking about me.

The dining room is different,
With table, chair and phone,
We once had 2 PC's,
But now we've only one.

The kitchen is full of dishes,
Which I am supposed to clean,
Even though I like water,
I think it's terribly mean.

The hall is very lonely,
It doesn't have any cares,
So if it doesn't have any,
I can jump across the stairs.

James Foster (10) Shade Primary School

MY RABBIT FLOPPY

I have a rabbit called Floppy,
Who has a comfortable bed,
And sometimes she escapes,
One day she banged her head.

One day she escaped,
And she was too fast for me,
I ran the fastest I could,
And I found her under a tree.

I crept up very slowly,
She took a turn about,
I quickly picked her up,
And I gave a happy shout.

Melanie Riley (9) Shade Primary School

MY GERBILS

My pet gerbil is called Jerry
At night he scratches in his cage
Sometimes I cannot sleep at night
Which makes me in a rage!
I used to have a gerbil called Joey
He used to run in his ball
But he escaped one terrible day
And was caught running down the hall.
I slowly crept towards it
It did not notice me
But it quickly turned around
Then it decided to flee.
Fortunately the door was closed
Meaning he's sort of in a trap
I caught him in my hands
And gave him a gentle tap.

Katy Knowles (10) Shade Primary School

WEATHER

I like it how the wind blows
And the sun shines brightly in the sky
But I wish I was a beautiful bird
Because I've always wanted to fly
I always hated the bad weather
It makes me soaking through
But it wouldn't really matter
If I was a little whale too.
I've always loved the windy gales
I think it is so fun
But I wish I was a tiny bird
So I could fly to the sun
Don't you just love the red hot sun
I think it is so nice
But it looks like a little red ball
With tons and tons of spice.
I hate the ice cold snow
I think it is so icy
It comes down in little white flakes
And looks kind of ricey
I like the soft white clouds
They really are so light
They can travel for miles and miles
Just like they were in flight
I hate the horrid dark clouds
I think they are so black
But I wouldn't mind if I was a bat
Because I could come flapping back.

Lisa Jane Whatmough (10) Shade Primary School

MY BROTHER

My brother is an awful pain
And whenever I'm in bed;
He grabs a cardboard box
And whacks me on my head.

And when it's time to get out of bed
I reach for a large old old gong;
And whack it with a coat hanger
So it gives out a loud *Dong!*

But I know he'll get me back
Cos he'll hide my wardrobe key;
He'll look so honest (he always does)
Then he'll come down to tea.

I'll do something, I really must
I think I'll play a trick;
In his bed I know
I place a candle stick.

Isabella Louise Uttley (9) Shade Primary School

ANIMAL POEM

I can be brown, black,
white and grey.
I have long legs
and soft they say.

I've got a long face
and eyes of brown
Most of the time I'm happy
it's unlikely that I'll frown.

They brush me down
every day
I can be wild
and be tame.

What am I . . . ?

Amy Gabrielli and Sophie Row (11) Stile Common Junior School

FLOWERS

Poppies remind us of something sad.
You see them in the field.
Flowers are my favourite things.
Flowers are really beautiful.
Flowers are many colours.
I love my garden.
In the winter,
When it is cold,
Badgers go there in holes as well
In spring flowers come up again
I love flowers
They are food for slugs and caterpillars
They are so beautiful nicer than worms
Or slugs, sunshine bright
They come from seed to bud
They smell like perfume blue, white, pink, purple and
yellow.
Graceful beautiful flowers.

Tracie MacKie (9) Stile Common Junior School

WHAT IS BLUE?

Blue is the sky
Blue are the bluebells
Blue is the colour of the salty sea
Blue is the colour of my eyes
Blue is the last colour in the rainbow
And blue is my favourite colour.

Faye Greenwood (8) Stile Common Junior School

SPRING

Daffodils, daffodils,
Towering high,
The blossoming trees stand
still in the sky,
The dew on the grass
trickles down the stem,
The spring is coming once again.

Michelle Atkinson (10) Sutton CP School

AUTUMN IS THE TIME

Autumn is the time when leaves turn red.
Autumn is the time when animals go to bed.
Autumn is the time when leaves drop to the ground.
Autumn is the time when the weather turns round.
Acorns, conkers, helicopters which fly,
Oak, chestnut, sycamore in sight.
Birds are on a very big flight.

Jody Currie (10) Sutton CP School

THE MONSTER

In the dark murky depths
Of the deep blue sea
There lurks a terrible monster
That can eat you and me

It swims around
And curls up in a ball
It's got twelve teeth
And could eat us all

So if you sail across the sea
And see an unusual sight
Please do hurry
It might just *bite!*

Georgina Ford (9) Sutton CP School

PUDDLES

Puddles, puddles
All around
Glistening raindrops
On the ground,
Grass so wet,
From the dew
Skies so grey
Dismal grey.

Caroline Mathers (9)   Sutton CP School

SNOW

Snow is falling drifting down
Falling gracefully on the ground
I built a snowman
A very white man!
Let's go sledging on the hill
Nearby the old, dusty, white mill
I'm getting cold
Very, very cold
I think I'll go home now
      Goodbye.

Claire Woof (9) Sutton CP School

WINTER

The snow is falling all around
Hurling, twirling to the ground
Everywhere as cold as ice
Slipping, sliding on the road
Noses red as a rose.
Our toes and fingers are very cold
Way through the wood a badger sleeps
Under a log a harvest mouse creeps
A prickly hedgehog wandering near
Wakes up when spring is here.

Steven Briggs (9) Sutton CP School

THE SNOWMAN

The snowman stands
As still as a stone
But when it gets warm
He starts to groan.
His nose falls off
And freezes on the ground
His hat falls off
He cannot see
His arm starts dripping
He cries, 'Help me!'
'Oh no,' he cries
My leg's come off
I'm almost gone
He dripped to death
As the sun shone.

Lee Briggs (9) Sutton CP School

AROUND THE WORLD

There was a boy called Jimmy Jay
Who jumped aboard a bird of prey
They flew all day and flew all night
Until they reached the break of light
They flew and flew a long, long way
Until they reached another day.
They flew over a rainbow
And over the sea
Around the moon
Until it dropped him
He fell and fell a long, long way
Until in a conifer he lay.

Emily Cummins (9) Sutton CP School

177

SPRING IS HERE

Hip, hip hooray, spring is here.
Hooray, hooray lambs are near.
Daffodils start to flower.
From the sun and rain's power.
Bees fly and buzz around.
Beetles crawl on the ground.
As quiet as mice, flies fly
Up, up high in the sky.
The wind blows as the flower grows.
Leaves grow on the trees.
Daffodils sway in the breeze.
How wonderful it is to hear.
Birds singing as clear as clear.
Let's all go and play out.
And laugh and laugh and shout and shout.
Birds come and make their nest.
Hedgehogs finish their winter rest.
Duck's eggs hatch.
A sweet, fluffy, little batch.
That hot summer's day would sometimes drift away.
I like to see children play.
Happily on this spring day.
How beautiful the world seems.
Lovely with its green scenes.

Lucy Eaton (9) Sutton CP School

GRANDMA

My grandma is old
She's 63
She never stops drinking cups of tea
She has a few wrinkles on her nose,
She sometimes has cottonwool between her toes.

My grandma is old
She's 73
She does not like cups of tea
But now she likes coffee
Especially with toffee.

My grandma is dead now
I miss her so much
I hope someday I will be
with her and we'll keep in touch.

Chloe Dearden (8) Sutton CP School

SUNFLOWER

Sunflower, sunflower
Always facing the sun
Turning, turning
Twisting, twisting
Growing, growing
Taller than the garden gate
Taller than the front door
Taller than the old tree
Wilting, wilting
Dying, dying
Getting smaller
Until you are gone.

Sam Riley (9) Sutton CP School

THE AUTUMN RAINBOW

The autumn rainbow is a colourful sight
With trees on fire with colours, bright
The fire is nothing but altered leaves
That drop in clusters from deciduous trees.
Floating above the still, silent pools,
Flies a great bird , the bright harvest moon.
The fruits of the harvest are locked in the barn.
While the cows eat the grass
Down on the farm.
The dew on the grass is like jewels in a chest,
The early bird chirps to its mate in the nest.
The fields are sparkling with bright silver frost.
When winter comes all this will be lost.

Katie Smith   (10)   Sutton CP School

THE NIGHTMARE

The vampire rises from the rocks,
Midnight strikes on all the clocks,
Heavy thuds stamp on the stairs,
Ghosts stalk the house in pairs.

Stones and clocks and toys and frocks,
Flying around the room,
Even a witch is flying up there upon her broom.

Martin Darnbrook   (9)   Sutton CP School

YELLOW

Bananas are - yellow
lemons are - yellow
sunny is - yellow
corn is - yellow
shiny is - yellow
lights are - yellow
daffodils are - yellow
buttercups are - yellow
and summer is the yellowest.

Mark Adams (9) Sutton CP School

THE BLUE DOLPHIN

The blue dolphin, fast and cute,
Her ears are sharp, her teeth are too.
With a slapping tail and a swishing fin,
That's the dolphin, that's blue, that's blue.

The blue dolphin swims the world,
It spins and plays with bottlenose too,
It jumps through the water up and down,
That's the dolphin, that's blue, that's blue.

The Blue dolphin likes the waves,
Crashing about with its tail and head too,
It's as long as a stick or even us,
That's the dolphin, that's blue, that's blue.

The blue dolphin, a water mammal,
It swims with her babies and family too,
Using its gills to breath so lively,
That's the dolphin, that's blue, that's blue.

Luke Argall (11) Sutton CP School

A WALK IN THE COUNTRY SIDE

I took a walk in the countryside and what did I see? I saw green
fields surrounding me.
As I went to a river where a stream ran by, I saw a tiny bird fly
up in the sky.
A walk in the countryside it has wonderful things to see, so why don't you take
a walk in the countryside and you'll see how
wonderful it can be!

Katrina Bower (9) Sutton CP School

THE PANDA

A black and white animal,
A lazy sleeper,
A slow mover,
A wet nose,
A bamboo cruncher,
A good climber,
A shy creature,
A bear-like animal,
A soft, furry body,
A relative of the racoon.

Victoria Mathers (11) Sutton CP School

AUTUMN

Autumn colours all around
Red, gold on the ground
Leaves crackle beneath my feet
Swiftly, softly they fall from trees
Landing in piles upon the ground
Covered with frost, silver shining on the leaves
Soon the sun will melt the freeze.

Gemma Hodgson (10) Sutton CP School

FLOWERS

Daffodils, daisies, roses too,
Grow in spring,
Just to greet you.

Trees and bushes,
Small and tall,
Grass all around you.

Brightly coloured petals,
On the flower tops.
Scattered all around you.
Summer, spring or not.

People doing gardens,
Planting flowers here and there,
Spring is here to greet you.

Laura Brickley (10) Swain House Middle School

MARY CRAVEN

She arrived in 1896
Mary Sudcliff was her name
then she married Arthur
and a Craven she became.

She was a Sally Army girl
as strong as one could be
she had a little daughter
Joany small and tender.

She had an exciting life
Before she turned one hundred
Then she went to Cliff Vale
where my mother used to work.

Elizabeth Routh (11) Swain House Middle School

THE TREES

Trees are gigantic
trees are green
trees are fun
and they are clean

There are lots of trees
big and small
full of bees
short and tall

There's different kinds of trees
different greens like lime, jade, olive.
They are made of different woods
they're like hoods.

Rajinder Singh (11) Swain House Middle School

SEASONS

Flowers blooming all around
sweet smelling flowers
springing from the ground

Romance in the air
new born baby rabbits
coming from their lair

The flowers wilt
leaves start to fall
all different colours falling to the ground

Winter near everything dull and grey
snowfall's now cold and wet
children playing, building snowmen.

Carly Harber (11) Swain House Middle School

WORLD

The trees look stunning
As they blow in the wind
The flowers look beautiful
and so bright
The grass is so comfy
But it looks bumpy.

The sun is so bright
And gives off so much light
The sky is so blue
Some parts a bird once flew
The clouds look like a new place
The world changes each day.

Christopher Carrigan (11) Swain House Middle School

SNOW

Snow, snow is so cold
cars frosted down the road
people wrapped up in warm clothes
snow, snow is so cold.

People playing in the snow
getting wet on the road
boys and girls throwing snow
snow, snow is so cold.

Snow, snow can be deep
people in their beds having a sleep
snow makes it so you can't see
snow, snow can be deep.

Ian Davidson (11) Swain House Middle School

MOUNTAINS

Top of the mountains the cold breeze blows,
Sitting there with a hot flask.
Not giving up until you've got to the summit.
Miles and miles of beautiful views,
Above the clouds the sun peeps through.
Down and down to the bottom,
Heavy rucksacks made of cotton..
Then at last we're near the end,
Goodbye, farewell my mountain friend.

Nicholas John Bose (10) Swain House Middle School

THE PARK

Trees are green
All different types of green:
Jade, khaki, lime, olive and other colours,
The grass is all different shades too.

Plants in assorted colours,
Pinks, reds, yellows
Contrasting shades,
Makes for a beautiful scene.

Birds flying high and low
Many varieties:
Blackbirds and sparrows,
Small ones and large ones.

Walking the dog,
Going for a picnic,
Feeding the ducks
And playing on the grass.

When a fairground comes along
We go on the rides,
Then hide from mum,
The park is such fun.

You can go today
And come back late at night
I like the park
It's the best place to go.

Gareth Shutt (11) Swain House Middle School

THE RACE

Run and run for miles.
Through the fields,
And over stiles.
Down the lane
And through the town.
Don't let the side down.

In the rain or even snow
Looking forward on you go.
It's too hot in the sun.
Listening for the starting gun. When it's breezy.
It feels quite easy.

There's the crowd to shout me on.
Can they see how fast I run?
Getting tired, feeling fine
Now I see the finish line
I might not win I'll do my best
One final push to beat the rest.

Leon Simon Bell (10) Swain House Middle School

FOOTBALL

I go to the stadium to watch them play,
It seems to me like it lasts all day.
1 o'clock, 2 o'clock, 3 o'clock, 4.
I ask my dad how much more?
On comes the physio, someone gets fouled.
The linesman laughed but the manager scowled.
Dad shouted come on and I started to moan,
But the whistle screeched and we all went home.

Richard Bohanna (10) Swain House Middle School

FADDY CAT

I'm fussing round
Purring loud
Surely it'll be tasty
Oh no!
It's out of a can
Cheap and nasty
and untasty.

It surely can't be edible
It's mushy, pasty and looks very
untasty.

What I would give for a slice
of that beef
succulent, juicy and in gravy.

If I plead and beg they'll
send me to bed
and my stomach will still be empty.

I'll go for a walk they'll
get out a fork they'll
tap it and worry, 'Where is he?'

But I'll turn a deaf ear
and disappear.

By morning that slice of succulent meat
will be there on my plate for me to eat.

Matthew Jas (11) Swain House Middle School

FOOTBALL

Football is my favourite game
Football is brill
I love things to do with football
I'm football crazy
I'm in Wembley going
in the dressing room at Wembley
Cheering them on
Putting their kit on
They are very confident
The manager shouts
Time to go lads
Pounding football boots
Through the tunnel
They're on the pitch
Stretching and straining
Waiting to start the match, the whistle blows
They're off, steady movements
Passing and crossing
Chipping it, twisting and
Turning, they are in the six yard box
Shearer blasts it from the
Penalty area, the keeper dives
He's too late, it's hit the post
The keeper made a mistake, he's stretching
His furthest, the ball goes
Clear the line, it's a goal
The whistle blows, it's full time.

Qasim Rehman (10) Swain House Middle School

MY HAMSTER

My hamster is called Nibbles,
He's got brown, silky fur and
cute round eyes.
I play with him all the time.
I feed him carrots and celery,
He chews at them frantically,
Eager for more.
Nibbles drinks from his bottle,
Sucking at it for water.
He exercises in his ball
like the ones on Gladiators.
He loves the mazes I make,
I place a trail of raisins down.
We have loads of fun together.
That's my hamster.

Karen Finter (9) Swain House Middle School

MUSIC

Pop music's fun,
Rock music's boring,
Pop music's OK,
But that's what I think.
Soul music's slow,
Tunes are good,
Country and western's alright.
But that's what I think.
Some sing in bands,
Some sing alone,
It's all good in a way
But that's what I think.

Katherine McBurnie (10) Swain House Middle School

PHOTOGRAPHS

My mum loves photographs
But only photographs of me
She puts them in the front room
For everyone to see.

When people see the photos,
They cry out 'Oh how sweet'
They cry out lots of other stuff
That I cannot repeat!

Photographs from June
Photographs from May
Photographs from Christmas
And from my last birthday

There are photos stashed away
Under mum's bed in a box
When me and friends look
We laugh lots and lots

Photos of when I was a baby
Photos of when my mum was young
Photos from when I did a play
Photos from when I sung

Photos from playing
Photos from school
Photos from halloween
When I dressed up as a ghoul

Photos from people moving house
Photos of good friends
Photos of making go-karts
Photos of making dens

In the world there's loads of strange photos
Where they'll go that's what no-one knows.

Amy Carrigan (10) Swain House Middle School

TEACHERS AND ME

I walk into school
there are teachers everywhere
Teachers in the playground
and teachers on the stair.

Teachers in the classroom
and teachers in the halls
Teachers in the staffroom
and teachers confiscating balls.

Then when the whistle goes
teachers line us up
We go into our classroom
where we all sit down.

Then Mrs Briggs, our form teacher walks in
'Sit down I say, children sit down'
Then we all sit down once again
she is very angry now.

Because Mark Johnson was messing about
with his pom pom ball on the reading couch
Mrs Briggs takes the register
but Mark is still messing about.

Then the buzzer goes for history
so we go to Mrs Lokory
She says, 'Our new topic is Egyptians.'
I wish I lived in Egypt, I said to Mark.

Then we worked on the jobs . . .
then the houses . . .
In the end the lesson ended
then the other lessons went fast.
The last buzzer went
Then I got out, yippee I say, yippee!

Jade Scullion (10) Swain House Middle School

193

ANIMALS

They jump up through the air,
With mud in their fur.
They swim in pools,
And act like fools.

Along the street they plod along,
Walking next to their master.
They do a jog and make it faster.
They do some things that make us laugh,
But we still love them and that is that!

Catherine Sanderson (10) Swain House Middle School

MY CAT

My cat is called Tiger
He always wants to play
He rolls around the garden
and that's where he likes to stay.

He likes to sleep on his back
In his favourite chair
But when my mum comes in
She gives him such a scare.

He followed my sister
Home from Hanson school
He always jumps around
In the paddling pool.

My cat is called Tiger
He's not a tiger as such
In fact he's totally black
But I love him very much.

Jennifer Moore (11) Swain House Middle School

SUMMER

In summer flowers grow
And all around the streams flow
Daffodils grow
And rose bushes are in bloom.

When the summer is over
Autumn comes
Leaves turn brown
And the trees go bare.

In winter the snow comes out
Children have snowball fights
And have lots and lots of fun
With their friends.

Sally Fowler (11) Swain House Middle School

SCHOOL DINNERS

School dinners are disgusting.
Vegetables and fruit.
They say they keep you healthy.
Why can't they give us something else,
Like chocolate, crisps, chips,
Buns and more chocolate.
They just slop lot's of food on your plate.
It's always the same things,
Broccoli, mash potato, peas and beans.
And the drinks,
It's always water.
Water and more water.
Why can't we have something else for a change.
Coke, Tango, that sort of thing . . .

Luckily I changed to sandwiches!

Paula Woollin (10) Swain House Middle School

195

NATURE

Nits gather round the lake,
Ants march in and out of holes,
There in the sky two ladybirds fell,
Under the ground one worm wiggled,
Running about on leaves two beetles fight,
Earth is full of nature.

Hannah Farnfield (8) Talbot Primary School

LIMERICK

There was once a guy named Stu,
Who desperately needed the loo,
So he went up the stairs,
But it was being repaired,
So he had to do it in his shoe!

Adele Hurst (9) Talbot Primary School

THE TROPICAL SEA

I looked into the tropical sea.
The waves crashing against the rocks,
Sounds like thunder in a sea storm.
Smashing, crashing, up and down.
Swirling, whirling, round and round.
The sea calms down so still.
You wouldn't think it was there.
All of a sudden it starts up again.
Smashing up against the rocks,
With bits of skeleton and fossils in it.
Smashing and crushing them up against the rocks.
Turning the skeletons into fossils.
Then it calms down again with not a skeleton in sight.
All of a sudden the sky goes all dark, dull and dim.
Shining yellow forks of lightning then, seconds later the thunder comes.
Sounding like elephants walking over our heads.
The sea goes crazy and keeps crashing and crashing.
Bits of skeleton and fossils flying everywhere.
Then all of a sudden the storm stops and the sea calms down.

Emma Victoria Brandwood (11) Thornhill J&I School

CAN'T SWIM IN THE POND

Water curled round me.
Fish tickled my toes.
I can only hear a light, trickling sound
Water swirled and twirled
The fountain shoots out water that delicately floats down.
Soon it comes winter
The pond ices up
Icicles hang from the window ledge
I stare out of my window at the pond
Can't swim in the pond
Can't splash, can't have fun
Can't go out, too cold
It's no fun inside.

Stacey Helliwell (10) Thornhill J&I School

CATS

Cats are all sorts of colours,
Like ginger and tabby and black.
I like it when they lick me best,
And when they snuggle up on my chest,
Or curl up tight on a winter's night,
Before the fire that's warm and bright.
And purr and sing, what joy they bring,
I've always wanted a cat.

Lauren Carter (9) Walton Junior School

LIVING THINGS

Living things come in all shapes and sizes
Purring cats and great big tigers
Pesky rats and bloodsucking bats,
Howling wolves and stamping hooves,
Barking dogs and leaping frogs
Little ants and a dog who pants,
Antelopes jumping down a slope
Polar bear and a running hare.

Living things come in all shapes and sizes
Spotty Dalmatians and fierce alsations
Poisonous snakes and handsome drakes,
Elephants with tusks and crowing birds at dusk
Harvest mice down a hole
Are sometimes joined by a black, velvet mole.
Big blue whale and a fish in a pail
Big red fox and a hamster in a box,
A grizzly bear and a very fast deer
A gerbil who is pleasant and a very fat pheasant,
Living things come in all shapes and sizes.

Laura Simonite (9) Walton Junior School

MIDNIGHT

At midnight,
When birds take flight,
Deep, blue sky,
Moon rising high,
The shining stars return to Mars,
The plants to sleep,
The mice arise to celebrate the night's surprise.

Emma Hudson (11) Wellington Middle School

THE CREATURE THAT LIVES IN THE SEA

There is a creature that lives in the sea,
With a very large eyeball in each knee.
Oh, what a marvellous swimmer is he!

(Splash, splish, splash, splash, splish)
(Splash, splish, splash, splash, splish)

This monster that loves being wet,
Will never be caught in a net.
Why? He's as big as a Jumbo jet!

(Splash, splish, splash, splash, splish)
(Splash, splish, splash, splash, splish)

This beast, oh he does love to eat,
On a Sunday his favourite treat
Is children's deep fried left feet!

Watch Out!

David Langwade (11) Wellington Middle School

THE MUSIC ROOM BAND

All the instruments make a band
All the instruments don't need a hand
The cello doing its very best
Well, so are the rest
The keyboard is so very shy
The violin says, 'why, oh why?'
The cymbals being quite quiet
Shame this isn't a *riot!*

Paul Bryar (11) Wellington Middle School

THE THING I HATE THE MOST!

Washing up, oh no
Ironing done, up stairs to go
Tidy room, not again!
Mum's yelling, what a pain!

Put out the rubbish,
bring in the milk,
asks mum with a voice of silk.

I think I've done,
so out to play!
Where do you think you're going?
You'll go when I say.

What about the bath?
Did you wipe the floor?
Just when I'd done, there's always
more, more, more.

Why me? I cry
When I want to play
Why me? I cry
When I've wasted a day.

I'm only eleven
I'm only a child,
If I can't go out,
then I'll turn wild.

So please mummy dear,
please be very kind,
employ me a cleaner,
so I can unwind.

So I can play out,
and have some fun!
'Cause I can't go out now,
until the cleaning's done!"

Alison Epton (12) Wellington Middle School

THE MONSTER UPSTAIRS

I feel so scared of the monster upstairs,
It yells at night and it screams in the light,
I feel so scared of the monster upstairs,
The neighbours next door are scared of us all,
because of the monster upstairs,
The monster upstairs creeps around,
When no-one's about and there is no sound,
The monster upstairs, so I've heard has
fifty-eight ears and toes.
Then one night I heard a noise,
But I wouldn't believe that it was
the monster upstairs,
So I told myself once, or maybe twice
it was just the wind howling down
the fireplace,
But I still feel so scared of the monster upstairs.

Adele Fieldhouse (11) Wellington Middle School

MAJOR

He never really speaks at all,
and yet he says so much.
His eyes are large and warm and brown
his coat is soft to touch.

He's happy with the simple things
like running in the fields
He knows some secrets yes it's true,
but his lips are always sealed.

If he's smacked or scolded
for doing something wrong,
you only have to say the word
and running back he'll come.

There was a time he ran away,
but he came back in the end.
Perhaps there's something we could learn
from watching man's best friend.

Katie Flathers (12) Wellington Middle School

MY AUNTIE MEG

If you know my Auntie Meg
You'll know she's got an extra leg!
People notice she's got three feet
When they walk past her in the street
She walks quite fast, sometimes slow
I'm telling you this 'cause you ought to know
I must admit she's strange but true
'Cause she's three legs instead of two.

My Auntie Meg has trouble with shoes
'Cause there's not many in threes that she can choose
And I suppose
She's got fifteen toes
(Five times three)
And it's weird having a relative
Not the same as you and me!

Jodie Crossland (10) Wellington Middle School

ON THE STREETS

On the streets in the dead of night
wishing I was in a house with a big bright light.
Sitting waiting for people to come
I want food, my fingers are numb.

On the streets begging for money,
people laughing - they think it's funny.
I go for a walk, everyone stares
It feels as if nobody cares.

On the streets, as cold as ever
people dressed in fancy leather,
throwing grubby pennies to me
I need love don't you see?

Kiranjeet Kaur (11) Wellington Middle School

MY VERY WEIRD FRIEND

It was weird all right,
his jumper was tight,
he had three arms in one sleeve at each side.

He had legs to match,
with a head that was thatched
and a lightbulb that shone out of each ear.

He had a green body,
with spots that were soggy
and very green fingers and toes.

And that was my friend,
very weird I suppose,
with eighteen fingers and toes.

Sara Hibbitts (11) Wellington Middle School

THE FLEA

I'm a flea,
And as happy as can be,
I run around on cats and dogs,
And suck their blood when they sleep like logs.

I once was on a dog called Spike,
Whose blood I really didn't like,
I left him for a Siamese cat,
Called Tommy Cooper, 'Just like that!'

I once lived on a police dog,
Who with the DI went for a jog,
He did his job at catching thieves,
But you should see all the food he eats on Christmas Eve.

I once was on a cat called Tigger,
And he just kept getting bigger,
He ate and ate all day and night,
And wouldn't give any away he was so tight.

I lived on an ugly rat,
And it ran about a flat,
It kept taking bits of food,
Then it got found out and sued.

Now I'm on a cat called Mog,
It gets chased by next doors dog,
It jumps up and falls off the fence,
Which proves it has no sense.

Gavin Stowell (12) Wellington Middle School

WINTER

Children playing in the snow,
Battling against winds that blow.
Old man tramping down the street,
Putting up with ice-cold feet.

Little children with boots so bright,
Glinting in the dim light.
Mouths blowing hot air,
Winter, winter everywhere.

Freezing fingers, freezing toes,
Walking against the wind that blows.
Snowball Jim and snowball James,
Try to ignore the very rude names.

Angry driver stops his car,
Walks back home from lands afar,
Freezing lips and freezing ear,
Now at last winter's here.

Bryony Betts (11) Woodend Middle School

BOYS!

They think they're cool,
They play a lot of pool
They think they're good
But they play in the mud

They are bad
They are mad
They are glad
But the girls are good

They play footie
They are nutty
They are lucky
But the girls are not

They are nice
They hate rice
They hate girls
But the girls are nice.

Samantha Wardle (11)   Woodend Middle School

PRETTY POLLY

My monster's different to yours
It's very nice and it's got big claws,
It's got long brown hair,
And it growls like a little cub bear.

Its nose is big and round,
It's like a potato stuck in the ground,
Its mouth is small,
Like a little boy's ball.

Its teeth are long and sharp,
But when they grind, they sound like a harp.
His breath smells like a big red rose,
Which puts everyone in a deep, deep doze.

His skin is fluffy and soft,
Like your teddy bear up in the loft,
His legs are long and fat
And at the bottom they are flat.

His feet are big like his claws
My monster's different to yours.

Daniel Hoyle (11)   Woodend Middle School

WILDERNESS

There is in me a sloth
quiet, slow but sure,
shy, yet thinking
what am I going to do?

There is in me a koala
watching as people go past
munching on leaves
sitting in the sun.

There is in me a hyena
laughing at people's jokes
and I am very silly
and very mischievous.

There is in me a parrot
who likes to talk
sits alone in front of the TV
repeating things that have been said.

Stuart Gray (11) Woodend Middle School

SCHOOL'S OUT

Girls scream
Boys shout
Children cry
School's out.

Cats run
Dogs shy
Into trees
Birds fly.

Teacher's glad
School's out
Teacher's happy
But how long

Old man
Hobble home
Merry minutes
Welcome home.

Racheal Ann Grogan (11)   Woodend Middle School

WINTER

Snowy days
Foggy nights
Cold ears
Red nose
Wintry showers
Snowball fights
Cars getting stuck
Wet, wet clothes
Foggy streets
I can't see
A thick cloth
Hanging in the air
Cold, cold ears
I have lost
my hat
Frosty roads
Cars slipping
Sliding, skidding.

Amanda Worrall (10) Woodend Middle School

THE BIG KIND MONSTER

As big as a house
not quiet like a mouse
strong as an ox
not sly like a fox
Gonzo the happiest monster

He grinned all day long
voice like a bird in song
had a passion for truffles
picked by hands just like shovels
Gonzo the happiest monster

He helped people out
going out and about
doing odd jobs
earning a few bob
Gonzo the happiest monster

One day he was glum
when a very close chum
couldn't get out of bed
'Cause of a pain in the head
Gonzo the happiest monster

But things soon got better
when receiving a letter
his chum was recovered
his pain was all smothered
Gonzo the happiest monster.

Amy Axon (11)   Woodend Middle School

PARENTS! FAMILIES!

I love my parents very much
I'll owe them till the day I die
even when I'm cooked in pie
I love them very dearly.

My dad, my mum
and sisters too
They are all a part of me
I love them very dearly.

I love them all
they love me
and that's the way that a family must be
I love them very dearly.

I love them all!

Danielle Phillips (10) Woodend Middle School

THE WILDERNESS

There is in me a dolphin
diving under water swimmer
Swimming different places diving back and fro.

There is in me a beaver
digging, rooting
Quick to move and do something else that's new.

There is in me a hamster
sleepy, drinking lots
Tired and sleepy during the day.

Amanda Fish (11) Woodend Middle School

MY LIFE ON A CANAL

Riding along in a big barge
See the scenery slowly passing by.
Carrying coal from here to there.
My daily meal is broth and bread,
I sleep under a thin blanket with Fred.
It's not a perfect lifestyle,
but it's not so bad.
After a while you get used to it.
When I first came to this barge it
wasn't very nice.
Ben was mean and Tess was harsh.
Now those days are in the past,
And I really love them.

Abigail Dewhirst (10) Woodend Middle School

BLACK

Black is the colour of the sky at night,
When all the stars are hidden out of sight.

Black is the colours of the bats hanging upside down,
Hiding in the towers down in the town.

Black is the colour of the witches cat,
That sits on the brim of the witches hat.

Black is the colour of the crow in the tree,
Who sits on a branch to see what he can see!

Samantha Wilson (10) Woodend Middle School

MY HORSE FOWLER

My Horse's name is Fowler
  he pulls the boat each day
We take our goods and drop them off
  when we're on our way
My lock-keeper's name is Robbie
  he opens the locks each day
We park our boat near the pub
  if we need a drink
When I go to the factories
  we always see families
They shout to us and wave to us
  when we're going to the factories
We carry coal for the boat
I sleep at the back of the boat
  where it's nice and warm.

Daniel Morrow (11) Woodend Middle School

THE PLAYGROUND

It's all very quiet in the playground, not a sound.
Then Ring! Ring! Ring! goes the bell.
Slam! Bang! go the drawers.
People chatter, chatter, chatter.
Clatter, clatter, clatter go their shoes.
They all run round in the rustling wind.
Screaming, shouting, they're all running round.
They're playing games and saying, 'You're out!'
People laughing and singing in the wind,
Then Ring! Ring! Ring! goes the bell,
They're all ready to go in.
Then the playground's quiet, not a single sound
sh sh sh!

Natasha Bux (10) Woodend Middle School

HAUNTED HOUSE

Haunted house, haunted house, haunted house.
In the haunted house's cellar . . .
Ghosts creep
Mice peep
Rats leap
And the bogeyman sits on the stairs.

In the haunted house's bathroom . . .
Spiders swim
Insects sink
And the cats drink out of the loo!

I'm not scared of that haunted house
No, not me
Ah! What's that behind me?
It's watching me . . .
It's waiting to pounce on me . . .
Ahh! It's the bogeyman!

Clare McQueen (10) Woodlesford Primary School

GONE!

Buzzy bee buzzy bee everywhere
Buzzy bee buzzy bee overthere
Buzzy bee buzzy bee don't go away
Buzzy bee buzzy bee gone!

Pussy cat pussy cat everywhere
Pussy cat pussy cat pulling my hair
Pussy cat pussy cat go away
Pussy cat pussy cat gone!

Grizzly bear grizzly bear everywhere
Grizzly bear grizzly bear eat a pear
Grizzly bear grizzly bear get out of the fridge
Grizzly bear grizzly bear gone!

Little girl little girl everywhere
Little girl little girl gone to the fair
Little girl little girl bored at the fair
Little girl little girl gone!

Eleanor Argyle (9) Woodlesford Primary School

THE TRUE STORY OF HAMLET

Hamlet's father was the king.
Claudius succeeded in killing him.
Now Hamlet's really mad!
Ophelia believes he's gone all bad.
One night Horatio had an awful fright,
Behind his back, he saw in the sky,
Hamlet's dad, flying high.
'Bring me Hamlet.' he said aloud.
Horatio brought Hamlet out.
'Who killed you father?' Hamlet said.
'While you were lying on your sunbed.'
'Now brace yourself and listen here,
Claudius poured poison in my ear.
Hamlet strode into the great hall,
Stared at Claudius, chunky and tall
'I challenge you to a duel.'
'I accept, you silly fool.'
In one quick moment Claudius was down.
And up Hamlet held the crown.

Lee Higgins & Martin Mullen (10) Woodlesford Primary School

SORRY I'M LATE FOR SCHOOL

I got attacked by a million men Sir!
They took me away to France Sir!
They threw me off a cliff Sir!
They made me swim to America Sir!
The waves were twenty foot high Sir!
I knocked that all out Sir!
Now can I go out to play Sir?

Shaun Impey (9) Woodlesford Primary School

SPRING

The cherry tree is unfolding its dainty buds.
The beautiful little lambs are resting in the woods.
I listen to the blue tits singing.
And nearby the church bells ringing.
Because spring is here.

I see the vivid green grass sway to and fro.
The farmers are ploughing the land ready to sow.
Daffodils are blooming
And the sun is blazing
Because spring is here.

Sorbet crocuses and lemon ones too.
See the sky so clear and blue.
Meadows with wild flowers gleam in the sun light.
The moon is shining in the night.
Because spring is here.

Kelly Dunmore & Rebecca Purt (10) Woodlesford Primary School

SPRING IS HERE

Spring is happy
The sky is blue
I walk by the canal to see the cherry tree bloom
The pussy willow, white like silk
I see the bird building a nest in the tree up high.
Spring is happy.
Spring is here.
The daffodils are golden.
Walk down the road to see the calf leaping with joy.
Spring is here.
The forsythia is golden as well.
The hedgehogs come out of hibernation to see the flowers and all.
Spring is here.

Hannah Ward (10) Woodlesford Primary School

ANIMALS I LOVE

Butterfly, butterfly I love you
See your wings, yellow and blue
Butterfly, butterfly I love you
I ask you to love me too.

Birdy, birdy can you fly?
What's it like up in the sky?
Birdy, birdy fly away I'll see
you tomorrow, all right, later today.

Animals, animals, what ever
You like, I'll be with you
day and night. Oh by the way
I love you still today.

Stephanie Walls (9) Woodlesford Primary School

EIGHTEEN AND NINETEEN

Eighteen and nineteen are a team
Eighteen and nineteen both wear jeans
Eighteen and nineteen eat raw peas
Eighteen and nineteen are like me.

Eighteen and nineteen are in their teens
Eighteen and nineteen are with me
Eighteen and nineteen come and see
Eighteen and nineteen are like me.

Eighteen and nineteen see me through
Eighteen and nineteen I see you
Eighteen and nineteen go to school
Eighteen and nineteen I love you.

Eighteen and nineteen I'm at school too
Eighteen and nineteen what are you
Eighteen and nineteen I still love you
Eighteen and nineteen I'm one of you.

Laura Sykes (9) Woodlesford Primary School

INFORMATION

We hope you have enjoyed reading this book - and that you will continue to enjoy it in the coming years.

If you like reading and writing poetry drop us a line, or give us a call, and we'll send you a free information pack.

Write to

Young Writers Information
1-2 Wainman Road
Woodston
Peterborough
PE2 7BU